Tithing

God's Intentions and Purposes

The quest for the truth...

John Okeke

"……. Wisdom is profitable to direct." In all your getting, get understanding.

It takes wisdom to get into the realm of God, and an understanding of His mind to know His ways. Reading of this book "Tithing: God's Intentions & Purposes" will not only bring an illumination into God's mind-set of the concept of tithing, but also helps one to understand the thought of God concerning them which is to cause their barn to be filled with abundance. Great book, Very Intuitive.

John Orji FHEA, PhD (C)

National Coordinator

UK Thanksgiving Day.

Tithes and offering and money issues will always be a challenge for Pastors because we do not want to cause offense. So I thank God for commissioning Pastor John to write a book on this highly contentious issue. The message in this book is clear, and insightful in the way the author balances God's instruction on payment of tithes and man's submission to the call of God. Everyone that reads this book will be glad they did.

Pastor Kemi Abidogun

General Overseer

Christ The Vine Church

Pastor John Okeke is a servant of God who teaches the WORD, with inspirational clarity and that manner of courage which is becoming all the more uncommon in these latter days.

In this book titled Tithing: God's Intentions & Purposes, Pastor John does not waste time propounding arguments that do not profit. Rather, he passionately and copiously draws from the unadulterated WORD of God, which is spoken by HIM for all ages.

The result: a totally compelling read and immersive experience, that opens up the mind of the reader to the realities of God's WORD as well as the eternal truism contained in Chapter 3 and Verse 8 of the book of Malachi "Will a man rob God? Yet ye have robbed me. But ye say, wherein have we robbed thee? In tithes and offerings".

I endorse this book and commend it to you all, for the edification of the Brethren and to the glory of God Most High.

Pastor John Okeke, I pray that God will use you as an effective and more effectual battle-axe in these end times, to uproot and tear down, to destroy and overthrow, to build and to plant."

Well done, Pastor.

Pastor FEYI OWOSENI
Christ The Vine Church

Contents

Acknowledgment

I want to acknowledge God the Father, God the Son and God the Holy Spirit for the inspiration He accorded me to be able to write this book, and I say, may His name be glorified in Jesus name. Amen!

Aims and objectives

The aims and objectives of this book is to take the Christian man or woman on a journey through the Bible to investigate the issue of tithe and come up with answers and clarity over it. Secondly, that through this book, there will be a lot more of its kind from the saints across the world regarding the subject matter through the revelation of the Holy Spirit so that God's name can be glorified

Introduction

"My heart is inditing a good matter: I speak of the things which I have made touching the king: my tongue is the pen of a ready writer." (**Psalms 45:1**)(**KJV**)

The controversy of tithing

The issue of tithing has caused so much controversy, confusion and division both from inside and outside the church. In my opinion, it has become the most debated doctrine of our time, and there does not seem to be any clarity whatsoever over this age long debate. So much attack has been hauled against Churches, General Overseers, Pastors and the likes, to say the least; from the social media which has become the pedestal platform from which the voices of the angry mobs, theologians, protesters, Bible scholars and disappointed church goers go to, to express their disappointments and disagreements. Most people you listen to on social media has argued that tithing is no longer applicable in our time. These Includes some prominent men of God who were supposed to know better. The surprising thing though is that it

3

feels some prominent Pastors and Ministers that used to be so vocal about the subject matter in the past, has suddenly lost their voices and has stopped saying much concerning this great Christian doctrine. Neither do they seem to have an answer to the people in defense of what they had held so dearly to, before now. The people are asking, show us the proof? Convince us by providing evidence that tithing is for New Testament believers? And all our G O's (General Overseers) and pastors has been able to provide is Malachi chapter three and the blessings attached to those who are obedient. Almost as if they feel the majority that are against tithing are right, and they themselves had been wrong all along, therefore they should just bury their heads in the sand and focus on other things that are of more important. But, who is right, and who is wrong? Are churches that collect tithes wrong to collect them, or are they right after all? Or are the disputers wrong in disputing it or are they right after all? Come to think of it, where is God in this conflict? I believe He is the only umpire in this issue; since the conflict is about Him. And surly, it is either those churches that collect tithes are right, or the disputers. There is only one outcome and I pray and urge you to read with open mind so you can make the decision at the end. And I pray that God should grant you clarity and better

4

understanding after reading this book
in Jesus name; Amen!

Chapter one: The ways of man verses the ways of God

"For my thoughts are not your thoughts, neither are your ways my ways, says the Lord. For as the heavens are higher than the earth, so are my ways higher than your ways, and my thoughts than your thoughts" **(Isaiah 55:8-9) (KJV)**

A few years ago, whilst posting tracts through letter boxes in a street in Accrington. As I walked along, I started to talk to myself about what would happen to those people whose homes I have posted tracks to, if by God's grace some of them should read the tract and decide to give their lives to Christ, and then pass away not long after: what would happen to their spirit or soul? They never for once in their lifetime set foot in church, never paid tithe and never gave any offering. What would happen to them? Would they still be saved? Will they make it to heaven, even though they never for once paid any tithe? Of course, they'll make it to heaven: another voice said within me. It is the faith in Jesus Christ that saves a man, not going to church or doing any of these religious rituals. As I battled with these thoughts in my head, I remembered an interesting session with my Sunday school teacher, a few months earlier.

6

I was fast asleep one fateful night when I heard a frantic knock at the door. "Who could be knocking at this ungodly hour of the night?" I muted to myself. I just hope it's not a decoy by robbers to get me to open my door, so they can rob me? Slowly I tip toed to the front door and peeped through the door hole to see who it was, only to discover it was my next door neighbour. When I saw him, all kinds of questions started to fill my head. What's happened to him? Is he being attacked? Who is he trying to escape from? Should I open or should I not open my door? After what seemed like eternity, I eventually opened the door. With tears in his eyes, he said his wife has not being able to sleep all through the night due to her health condition and that the situation has gotten out of control, so he came to ask if I could lend him some money to take her to the hospital: otherwise she might not make it till morning. The moment he mentioned money, I was like someone incapacitated. I would have loved to help but the only money with me was the money I had previously set aside as my tithe, to be given on Sunday to church. Surely, no way I'm giving my neighbour the money that belong to God. "What do I do, at this situation?" I asked my Sunday school teacher.

If I give this money to my neighbour to help save his wife's life, God will

7

be pleased that His money has been able to save a poor man's dying wife. Do I still need to pay this money back to God, even though I've already done the work of a Good Samaritan? "Well," he said. "But you'll still need to pay it back plus a twenty percent interest. That is what the bible said." "If you want to buy back the Lord's tenth of the grain or fruit, you must pay its value, plus 20 percent" (**Leviticus 27:31**). (NLT) "Twenty percent interest!?" I exclaimed. "But sir that will not be fair! God desires mercy not sacrifice, and I'm sure He's not going to ask me to pay back the tithe, let alone adding a twenty percent interest to it. He is not a wicked God!" I argued with my teacher.

Before we proceed any further, I would like to stress that a lot of people have recently come up with a lot of arguments as to why Christians are no longer required to pay tithes. Some of these arguments will be discussed after laying some basic foundations. Also, I would like to emphasis that some of these arguments sound beautiful, especially the ones that claim that Christ paid the price by delivering us from the curse of the law. That is true, and nothing can be done against the truth, but for the truth. It is a good thing to use the word of God to make cases for God, which is what most people that has argued, had done, whether it is clear

8

to them or not. However, who among the sons of men, can successfully defend, or make a case for God? Please note, the person we make a case for, to defend is the same one whose Spirit wrote every line of the Bible. Including the full stops, the comas, the colons, the semi colons as well as the question marks. No matter how much a person may know about God and His Word, they only know in parts. Hence, the Bible says,

"Prophecy and speaking in unknown languages and special knowledge will become useless. But love will last forever! Now our knowledge is partial and incomplete, and even the gift of prophecy reveals only part of the whole picture! But when the time of perfection comes, this partial things will become useless" (**1 Corinthians 13:8-10**) (NLT)

It is good to make arguments for God and try to defend Him. But we must be careful when doing so. Lest at any time, we ourselves become guilty and snared by the same person we are trying to defend. This what happened to Job's friends. They defended God and thought they knew better; but at the end, they were found guilty and had to be prayed for, else face the wrath of the very person they were defending and making a case for.

What I will try to do in this book is to use the Word of God to throw some light and understanding on the issue of tithing, which has literally become the great debate of our time.

So much has changed within the past few decades. More so, with issues regarding modern day Christians and tithing. People's views and mindset have shifted from the quiet and obedient sheep they used to be, to that of analytical, critical, angry and disobedient towards the man on the pulpit. The key reason for this been that the lifestyle of the man on the pulpit has been weighed and scrutinized against the lifestyle of Jesus Christ that many of them claim to represent, and they have been found wanting. As a result, there has been a silent revolt which has gradually metamorphosed into an all-out war between those in the virtual world, against those in the pulpit of some Churches. Indeed, there has been a lot of 'falling away' which the Bible warns against clearly. There is also no doubt that the devil has intensified his deceitful attacks against the Church of God by causing many to turn away from using the life style of our Master Jesus Christ as an example. He has also instilled the spirit of greed and worldliness in them, and no doubt, has planted some fake Pastors as well. By so doing, God Himself has to expose them to the whole world to see. The result of that exposure is that all kinds of doctrines and interpretations has cropped up, which are inconsistent with the message of our Lord Jesus Christ.

In addition, a huge number of people have suddenly become preachers in the virtual world; not without their personal interpretation and views about the Word of God, instead of carefully and diligently seeking to know God's own interpretation. The Bible says in **John**'s gospel **chapter 4:24** that "God is a Spirit: and they that worship Him must worship Him in spirit and in truth." The things of God are spiritual and mysteriously incomprehensible to the carnal man. I believe that many people that argue about the legitimacy of tithing, ever sat down to humbly study and seek the understanding of the Holy Spirit on the issue. Instead, what they do is listen to hearsay, and run with whatever they hear, if it sounds good to their ears: without taking the time out themselves to seek the knowledge that is needed by themselves.

Thus, I want to ask you this question before we proceed: what is your take on tithing? Are you in support of tithing, but are now beginning to have a second thought due to the logic and interpretations of people in the social media? Or are you one of those that strongly disagree,

and nothing can change your mind
otherwise?

Chapter two: Tithe, God's or man's ordinance?

There is no doubt or confusion about who ordained for God's children to pay tithe in the Old Testament. However, the problem many are facing today is that the time has passed because we are now in the New Testament. An era of grace and that Christ already paid every price required by the law, including tithing. Some will go on to say the only financial obligation against the believer are his offerings and, or helping the poor and the needy. Others on the other hand would argue that Ministers of God misappropriates the tithes of the people by using it to live lavishly: therefore, it made no sense to give their hard-earned money to such Ministers. Others would go on to say our Lord Jesus never say yes or no; therefore it is not relevant.

The above are some of the views of people; however, in the New Testament, there is no where we find Jesus nor his disciples imply we are not to pay tithe. Instead, every argument against, has been based on opinion and personal judgment.

Almost with tears in my eyes as I write this book, and a sense of regret that some of our generals, those we look up to in all our different

Assemblies, appeared subdued to the extent of not having the strength and courage to stand and give a clear support to what they had initially believed in, that made them who they are today. I feel disappointed to say the least. How can we just surrender as if we were never sure ourselves in the first place? What stops us from digging deeper into our Bibles and coming up with answers to this situation? Did some of our generals conclude they're right? Are the disputers right? What is your view?

You who say we are no longer under the law, do you observe any part of the law? For example the Ten Commandments which says you shall not steal, lie, swear or kill? Are these not all part of the law God gave Moses? Why do you honour them as a Christian if we are no longer under the law? The reason you honour these laws is that God commanded you to honour them not necessarily because they are laws that appeal to you to honour. Is this not the same with tithe and offerings? Those who argue we should not pay tithe do not argue we should not give our offerings. The reason been that offerings are free will whereby a person can decide to put a penny inside the offering basket without feeling guilty, as opposed to the guilt one has when they do not pay their full tithe. The funny thing is, people do not have an issue with dropping penny's into the offering

14

basket because they think they're obeying God's command to give. But they forgot that when God said "you are robbing me in offerings" He did not just mention offerings but also mentioned tithes. Tithes and Offerings. So you see, one cannot do one and neglect the other. Which was what Jesus told the Pharisees; they do one thing and leave the other things undone.

Chapter three: The Wisdom of God

"Because the foolishness of God is wiser than men, and the weakness of God is stronger than men" **(1 Corinthians 1:25)**

There is one word to describe those who are outside of the church (e.g., the unbelievers or non-Christians) that word is what the Bible described as lack of "fear of God." In fact, the Bible went on further to describe them as fools in **Psalms chapter 14:1**. I would personally take offence if somebody comes to me and calls me a fool inferring that is what their Bible says concerning me. But guess what? It is exactly what God calls them. The reason for this, is possibly because every handwriting of creation attests to God's existence. Everything about mankind and the human race points to God's existence; but yet, even though they know about these things and about God's existence, they still chose to deny Him. Not only did they deny Him, they would still go as far as condemning Him and saying all manner of evil against the Creator of the universe. Here is what the Bible says concerning them;

"For the wrath of God is revealed from heaven against all ungodliness

16

and unrighteousness of men, who hold the truth in unrighteousness; because that which may be known of God is manifest in them. For the invisible thing of him from the creation of the world are clearly seen, being understood by the things that are made, even his eternal power and Godhead: so that they are without excuse: because that, when they knew God, they glorified him not as God, neither were thankful: but became vain in their imaginations, and their foolish heart was darkened. Professing themselves to be wise, they became fools." (**Romans 1:18-22**)

Now, people outside the Church walls can say all manner of things concerning and against the Godhead and His doctrines because they lack the fear; neither do they have a clue of what judgment awaits them if they fail to repent. But what about believers and their attitude towards God? I fear because the same word spoken above concerning unbelievers can be said concerning some believers of this generation.

Many believers of our day have become more enlightened and more potent than the Creator of the Universe, to even dare to override His Doctrine, either consciously or unconsciously: without fear of what He may or may not do to them. (The **Bible** says we should fear God but nowadays

17

we have lost the fear of God completely, all in the name of grace.) I am very careful with the phrase, 'what He may do to them' as I'm aware it might not go down well with some people who will say, here we go again. As some had previously said 'if we don't pay our tithes, we will not make heaven' and this statement to them is blasphemy. And I agree with them to an extent.

Christ has paid the price of sin for the world. Nothing can surpass what the Lord did in-terms of salvation. However, I personally believe there is more to tithing than the money involved. Tithing goes deeper than what we know; the money involved in tithing is not the issue, but the obedience behind tithing that matters. This is why it is important we pay attention to what is said by the Almighty God instead of being carried about by every wind of doctrine been preached by men.

One thing I have come to understand in all my years of being a Christian is this; men will always have personal understanding and rhema, as you would call it, which at the long run, influences their judgment and interpretation of the Word of God. Another thing I've come to understand with men is this: there is a place in the human mind that loves to be praised and acknowledged. You can call this pride or ego. This place prides itself with knowledge and how much revelation it has concerning a subject matter. As a result, men wants to be seen as the ones with the most revelation. He wants to be looked upon as the man out of whose mouth proceeds those words never before spoken. So that when he speaks, there is a lot of excitement and applause from his audience.

However, this is a dangerous place to be for a man or woman that has responsibility to discharge the message of The King. Because, come to think of it, how much excitement is there in the Word of the King towards His subjects who are always on the lookout to find an excuse not to execute the Word of the King? King Saul was in this position during his time as the King of Israel. Hear what the prophet said to him,

"And Samuel said, hath the Lord as great delight in burnt offerings and sacrifices, as in obeying the voice of the Lord? Behold, to obey is better than sacrifice, and to hearken than the fat of rams. For rebellion is as the sin of witchcraft, and stubbornness as iniquity and idolatry" (**1 Samuel 15:22-23**). (KJV)

In the above passage, one cannot mistake what is more important to God between sacrifices and obedience. Every believer knows how important it is to obey in true Christendom. We learn this in the Sunday schools, Bible studies and in Bible schools that with God, obedience is better than sacrifice. But this word no-longer has any meaning in some modern Churches; which is why you find people in Church for decades and yet, still comfortable with their old habits and lifestyles. Many Christians gossip in Church, tells lies in Church, fornicates, and commits adultery in Church. In some Churches you find both armed robbers, murderers and occultists lifting up their hands in worship to God; despite knowing the Bible warns against such; that those who engages in such activities will not inherit eternal life: but yet they care less about the Bibles warnings because they lack the fear of God in them.

I must say this; some people think the law is bad that was why God had to change it. But nothing can be further from the truth. The law is not bad. Why would a loving God give us what is bad? The law is perfect but the only problem is that no man was able to satisfy its demands. The only person able to satisfy the law is our Lord Jesus Christ which is why he became the end of the Law of 'Righteousness', and became our Righteousness. The question would be, why does he need to satisfy the law and pay the price that is required, if the law is bad? The answer is clear. The law is not bad but incredibly excellent. Which is why today, if any man still chooses to take its route in finding God instead of through Jesus Christ, they are more than welcomed to try; and if they succeed, they will still see God. But this is not possible and my advice is, "do not try it, you will not succeed if you do."

"For Christ has already accomplished the purpose for which the law was given. As a result, all who believe in him are made right with God. For Moses write's that the law's way of making a person right with God requires obedience to all of its commands." (**Romans 10:4-5**) **(NLT)**

The only difference between the Law and Grace is that the Law was our School Master, who punishes us when we disobey. The Law does not show mercy or pity. Whereas Grace on the other hand forgives us when we disobey and err against God. In the Law, all the rituals they were required to perform, did not made them righteous including that of paying the tithe, the same thing is Grace. Everything we are doing or asked to do, or not to do does not make us righteous either. And that includes the tithes and offerings or any other works we think we are obliged to do as Christians. Brethren, the entire Bible is the Law of God whether

21

Old or New Testament and no man can meet the demands of God, not even the angels but Christ alone.

So do not think paying or not paying your tithe has anything to do with your salvation. Which is why we can still pay them and still end up in hell because it is detached from the issue of salvation, or righteousness as the Bible describes it in the above text. Both the Law and Grace teaches us one thing, which is to be good, (to be good in this context means to be righteous) and no man can be righteous by simply paying or not paying tithe.

No man can be righteous by merely not committing adultery or fornication, by not stealing or not committing murder etc. So what then is the problem, since it's got nothing to do with salvation? Why then should I pay it? Well, here's the problem, 'Disobedient.' Disobedient is refusing to act upon what God demands we do, and doing what He forbids us to do. Everything we know and observe today as Christian morals came out from the Law. For example, it is the law that warns us not to take what belongs to others, stealing. It is the law that warns us not to fornicate or commit adultery. It is the law that warns us to honor our Parents, it is the law that forbids us from bowing or worshipping other gods, and it is the law that warns men should not have sex with their fellow men as they would with women. The same law is what warns us not to have sexual intercourse with our siblings or parents with children. It is the law that warns us not to swear or profane the name of the Lord and so many other laws we hold as doctrines today as children of Grace.

If I as a Christian, goes on to deliberately break any of these laws, what does that make me? Disobedient. And we cannot justify our actions by saying we are children of Grace, therefore we are no longer bound by these laws because it is the Old Testament Laws. No! We cannot do that. That is why Apostle Paul said in **Romans chapter 6:1-2** "What shall we say then? Shall we continue in sin, that grace may abound? God forbid. How shall we, that are dead to sin, live any longer therein?" So you see, we cannot continue to break any of God's word whether in the Old or in the New Testament just because we are children of Grace, and still expect grace to abound. Thus, if this is the case with other issues that come under the law, why should it be different with tithing? Are we choosing and picking to do only what suits us and discarding the ones that displeases us?

'Christ is the end of Righteousness for those that believes.' Brethren, as far as God is concerned, no man can attain righteousness, no matter how hard they try. Righteousness can only be given as free gift. However, once we are given the cloak of righteousness to put on, we become part of a unique Kingdom, the Kingdom of God. And there are things that we are required to do as Citizens of the Kingdom, and these requirements is where the requirement to tithe falls under. I have not yet seen any kingdom or country whereby its citizens are not expected to behave in a certain way or are not expected to abide under some certain codes or conducts.

If the kingdom of man is so, why do we think the Kingdom of God will be any different? Let me expatiate a little further. I came to live in the UK as an immigrant until I was dimmed fit to have met the requirements to become a British Citizen. The very day I was declared a British Citizen, I started to enjoy all the benefits and privileges every British Citizen enjoys. However, there are still UK laws that I must abide by, and any day I break any of these laws I am prosecuted and if I am found guilty, I will be sent to prison. The UK Prime Minister or the Queen will not say "Do not put him in prison because he is a UK Citizen." I will be sent to prison. And if it is a country like America and my offense is the type that warrants death sentence, I will be put on death row to await my execution day. This is how it is in the Kingdom of God as

well. You break the rule God will
chastise you. And if your offense is
such that demands a death sentence,
nothing will save you; unless God
grants you mercy to repent before you
die and avoid eternal death. Why?
Because the rules and laws are there
for all to see.

Chapter four: The law, in the context of Apostle Paul's admonition to the Galatians churches

"Study to show yourself approved unto God, a work man that needs not be ashamed; rightly dividing the word of truth" (**2 Timothy 2:15**)

Before we proceed any further, it will be worth highlighting some of the points most people raise to support their decisions not to pay tithe. They say things like;

I cannot pay tithe, I don't have enough money. I can't pay tithe because it is been misappropriated by Pastors and General Overseers. I can't pay tithe because it is an Old Testament law that Jesus delivered us from. My tithe belongs to me because God said I should eat my tithe. I cannot pay tithe because Jesus was neutral on the issue. I cannot pay tithe because all I am expected to do is to give a freewill offering.

Here's my question; what is the worst thing that could happen, if assuming these statements are right? Let's say it is true, we are no longer required to pay tithes as a result of what Christ did on the cross, and still blindly or ignorantly continues to pay, nonetheless? What is the worst thing that could happen in terms of our relationship with God? Will the Lord go on to remit it as sin to us saying we are not supposed to pay it, therefore we have committed sin in doing so? Or will He commend us at the end of the day for going above and beyond what is required of us? On the other hand, what if you are wrong? What if everybody is wrong? What if God truly demands our ten percent after all, and we refuse to pay our due? What do you think will happen, in terms of our relationship with Him? Will He reprove, or commend us? Will He hold us guilty or will He congratulate us all the same? What is your answer to these questions? What is the worst thing that would happen if we go beyond what is expected, or if we fall short of the least of that which is expected of us?

"Christ has redeemed us from the curse of the law, being made a curse for us: for it is written, cursed is everyone that hangeth on a tree: that the blessings of Abraham may come on the gentiles through Jesus Christ: that we might receive the promise of the spirit through faith." **(Galatians chapter 3:13-14)**

Why is this passage not written; Christ has redeemed us from the curse of the law that the blessings of God or of Jesus Christ may come to the gentiles? Why blessings of Abraham in the Old Testament? What has Abraham got to do with the blessings since Christ died and delivered us from everything that's to do with the Law as some claim?

This passage did not say "Christ has delivered us from the Law," no! Instead, "Christ has delivered us from the curse of the Law." These are two different things. Laws are just rules and regulations that is expected of any people. Everybody no matter who they are or where they may be, has laws under which they abide to. Without laws governing us, this world would be an uninhabitable place due to the wickedness of men. What we should be asking is, what is the curse of the law, and what is the blessings of Abraham? Because; clearly, Christ delivered us from a curse, not from the law itself. Two things are distinctively clear in this passage, these are, 'CURSE AND BLESSING.'

What exactly is the law? It is important to understand first, and foremost what the law is. Secondly, why God gave it to Moses to give to the people? And thirdly, what it was meant to achieve? So, what does the law look like? When we say the law, is the law itself beautiful or ugly from the stand point of both God and man? If we do not first understand what the law is,

28

from a moral point, it becomes very easy for us to castigate, condemn and disassociate ourselves as far as we can from it, if we fail to grasp its worth. And to do an excellent job, it will be a great idea to first identify the Law Giver. And the Law Giver, though Moses handed it to the people, it was actually God that gave it to the people by proxy through Moses. Moses never invented any law by himself, instead, they were all handed down through him. Take for example the law of the Ten Commandments. The law was not designed by man who is evil, but by God who is excellently perfect beyond everything we understand to be perfect. Is it possible that a loving God can give what He knows to be evil to His people? Of course not. Every good and perfect gift is from God. The Bible says, "If we men that are evil know how to give good gifts to our children, how much more shall our heavenly Father give good gifts to them that ask him?" **(Matthew chapter 7:11)**

So, let's start by saying that the law was designed to instruct, teach, reprove, guide, discipline, admonish and attract reverential fear of God. It was designed to steer people away from evil and steer them towards honouring and reverencing God instead. It was designed to teach people the importance of loving one another, instead of living in enmity. Even the New Testament teaches us that,

29

"... All scripture is given by inspiration of God, and is profitable for doctrine, for reproof, for correction, for instruction in righteousness: that the man of God may be perfect, thoroughly furnished unto all good works" (**2 Timothy chapter 3:16-17**)

To understand the law, one must begin from the point and perspective of God. The summary of the law is that God is Holy and cannot behold sin. What is sin? Sin is anything that is displeasing to the Father. For example: God loves everybody. Nobody comes into this world with the hate of God on them. On the contrary, every human being no matter the circumstances of their birth, came into the world with the love of God on them, until they chose and decide for God not to love them.

Because God loves every human being, He expects us to love one another as well as ourselves just as He does to us. And anytime we fail to demonstrate this love, it becomes a sin, why? Because, God is displeased. Over ninety percent of the law is about human relations. And the remaining are the ones directly related to God, such as; we must not have any other god besides Him, we must not blaspheme the Holy Spirit, and we must not swear. So you see, everything about the law is about loving, and being fair towards our fellow man and to ourselves as well.

That been said, how can we claim the law is bad or evil? Something designed for the betterment of the people? The only problem is that man is evil, and cannot do right to himself, or to his fellow man. Not because the law is bad and must be removed. The Laws of God will never be removed neither will God reduce His standard because of man's inability to do what is right.

Here's the Law; God is Holy, and Just. Anytime He sees anything contrary, He eliminates without hesitation. Therefore, so as not to destroy His people when they commit sin, He gave them some written rules to remind them how not to displease Him, so He does not destroy them. (Displeasing another human being is to displease God) To the people, it is the law of God, but to God, it is His righteous judgement. It is His way of getting us to love and do what is right to one another. The law is the righteousness, holiness, love and mercies of God towards his children in manifestation. To say that the law is bad is to say our God is bad. Before we condemn the law, we must first ask ourselves what part of the law is bad.

What is the curse of the law? The curse of the law which Christ delivered us from is the tit-for-tat, an eye for an eye, the soul which sins must die without mercy in the front of two or more witnesses' mentality and practice. The stoning to death of the guilty and the endless ritual of the sinner in an attempt for their sins to be forgiven. This is what Christ delivered us from. Christ did not deliver us from doing what is right, and we know the law contains what is right. Christ did not deliver us from committing adultery or from lying, so we can carry on committing them. What He delivered us from was the death sentence appended to everyone who is guilty by breaking the law and the notion or belief that when we obey these instructions of the law, it makes us holy and blameless before God. Which is why the Bible says:

"...For by the works of the law, shall no flesh be justified" **(Galatians chapter 2:16: Romans chapter 3:20).** Why is that so? So no flesh will boast in God's presence by saying 'I earned my salvation as a result of my hard work.' No! No amount of hard work can save us, only faith in Jesus Christ. That does not mean we should not do any work simply because works does not justify or save us.

In the dispensation of the law, when a man commits sin, he goes to the High Priest with the required animal with which the priest makes an atonement with; and sprinkles the blood of the animal on the person and their sins were forgiven them. The Bible says without the shedding of blood there is no forgiveness for sin. The next time the man commits another sin, he does the same thing he did previously, and this ritual goes on and on, as long as the individual is alive. Also, depending on the type of sin committed. Some sins have death penalty, once you are caught, you're done for. Such as when a woman is apprehended in the act of committing adultery.

The reason the offender goes each time with an animal for his offense to be forgiven is because the blood of those animals could not pay the price of sin; which is death. Because, the soul that sins must die. So in effect, what happens each time a person goes in with the blood of an animal for the remission of his sin was an exchange of life. He exchanges his life with that of the animal. Therefore, instead of him dying, the animal dies in his place. But, here is the problem, the blood of those animals was not potent enough to atone fully for the sins of a human being. It is not possible. Otherwise, one might as well exchange human life each time with an animal's life and there will not have been the need for Jesus to come and die for us.

If it had been animal to animal it would have been understandable, but an exchange of animal to human being was more or less a mockery in respect of how precious the soul of a human being is before God. However, there was no other way out during that era because the time for Jesus to be revealed had not yet come. Thus, God had to implement that sacrificial process as a temporal measure, until the arrival of the true Lamb of God which is Jesus Christ. Only His blood is able to cleanse the sins of the entire world through one single sacrifice. Thereby, sparing the needless deaths of millions of animals which God created for a different purpose. I want to believe that every sacrifice made in the Old Testament by the blood of bulls or rams, all the human lives they were used to atoning for, must have been kept aside by God, waiting for the time our Lord Jesus had to take His own blood to the Father to wash all those Old Testament souls. The Father must have done a back dating of soul cleansing in other to accommodate the saints of the past after the death of our Lord Jesus.

The blessings of Abraham on the other hand is that the sinner no longer needs to bring an animal sacrifice in other for his sin to be forgiven. He does so by faith in the Son of God. Hence, why the veil of the temple got torn in two when Jesus died, was so we can enter boldly into the Holy of Holies without restriction. So the law or works within the context of Apostle

Paul's message to the Galatians, is any attitude, doctrine, tradition or ritual that is adopted, exhibited, displayed or practiced with the notion they are the things that save us, rather than what Jesus had already done on the cross for us. The curse of the law is a thing of the mind as opposed to the written word. That is why, what brought about Apostle Paul's exposé was the fact that the Galatian Church wanted to go back to physical circumcision; probably as a result of Apostle Peter's initial actions before being challenged by Paul; Instead of the faith in Jesus Christ. (**Galatians chapter 2:11-18)**

Chapter five: Laying the foundations

A question to those who say the time of tithing is long past. Has the time of God's covenant of peace and mercy over your life passed? Do you use any part of the Old Testament to pray? If yes, what makes you think they will work for you since you claim some passages are no-longer relevant for the Christians of this generation? Why do we claim the blessings of Abraham if we cannot follow Abraham's footsteps? Most of our arguments are from **Galatians 3:13** that Christ has redeemed us from the curse of the law; however, we fail to connect from the preceding verses, and here is what the preceding verses say, starting from verse six;

"…Even as Abraham believed God, and it was counted to him for righteousness." (My emphasis). Abraham heard the word of God and believed without questioning or trying to rationalise the instructions given. Abraham's attitude is, if God utters a word, I will believe and run with whatever is said, without question. Why? Because he judged God faithful. (Is God still faithful, or has He lost

His faithfulness over the years? suppose we too can come to the same resolute point where Abraham got to, and judged God to be faithful. If we do, we too would stop trying to rationalise what God says in the past: or adding words in His mouth by implying, He said what He never said). Abraham believed what God was doing at that moment in his life, and what He said He would accomplish in him, in the future. Because Abraham believed God, he would go on to do everything God asked him to do. Including sacrificing his only son Isaac, to demonstrate his obedience, should God permit him. Today, following Abraham's footsteps, how far would you go for God? Will you go the extra miles or would you rather stand on the fence instead?

"…Know ye therefore, that they which are of faith, the same are the children of Abraham" (**Galatians 3:7**). **(KJV)** The New Living Translation puts it this way: "The real children of Abraham, then, are those who put their faith in God." (My emphasis). They which are of faith are the children of Abraham. We are the children of Abraham today because we are supposed to be doing, or are required to do the same thing Abraham did over five thousand years ago. We are linked with Abraham, not with the law that would come over four hundred years after Abraham. We are of faith because Abraham the Father of faith, gave birth to us spiritually, and as such, we ought to do the same things Abraham did. Jesus said to the Jews, "Verily, verily, I say unto you. The Son can do nothing of himself, but what he seeth the Father do: for what things soever he doeth, these also doeth the Son likewise" **(John 5:19) (KJV)**

Abraham paid tithe and the Bible emphasised that Levi, who would later collect tithes from his brethren, also paid tithe whilst in the loins of his father Abraham. The reason for **Hebrews 7:9-10** is to enlighten us that Abraham's off springs were expected to pay tithes, and they did pay. Thus, we also that are claiming to be Abraham's children are also expected to do as our father did, and Jesus himself showed us that everything he did was the things he saw the Father do. "I speak that which I have seen with my Father: and ye do that which ye have seen with your father. They answered and said unto him. Abraham is our father. Jesus said unto them, if ye were Abraham's children, ye would do the works of Abraham" **(John 8:38-39) (KJV)**. The verse 39 of this passage goes this way in the New Living Translation; "…our father is Abraham!" they declared. "No" Jesus replied, "For if you were really the children of Abraham, you would follow his example.

Therefore, if Abraham is our father of faith as we are claiming him to be, then we must do the works of our father. Even our Lord Jesus is asking us to do the works our father Abraham did because he is the father of faith. If there is no significance and correlation of what Abraham did with us, why would his actions come to hunt us five thousand years later: that Apostle Paul would dedicate a portion of his time to lecture us about its implications? Have you thought of that?

"…And the scripture, foreseeing that God would justify the heathen through faith, preached before the gospel unto Abraham, saying, in thee shall all nations be blessed" (**Galatians 3:8**). **(KJV)** "…What's more, the Scriptures looked forward to this time when God would make the Gentiles right in his sight because of their faith. God proclaimed this good news to Abraham long ago when he said, "All nations will be blessed through you." **(NLT)** (My emphasis). The Omnipresent God, knew what He wanted to do to the children of the dispensation of grace, being us, the children of faith. Went ahead and preached the same Gospel we are hearing today to Abraham. The Bible recorded that Abraham, after hearing the Gospel believed. Question, when did this take place? The same passage where he gave tithe to Melchizedek in **Genesis 14:17-20**, and at different times He visited Abraham to give him the promise.

Thus, Abraham's tithe would go on to be a direct response to the same Gospel we are hearing today. Another question. If the tithe issue is exempted from the children of this dispensation because we are under Grace. That was the same grace Abraham would have been in, when he first received the Gospel and got certified righteous. Why was he required to pay tithe after hearing the Gospel we claim disqualifies us today from paying tithe? Suppose Abraham believed God and got justified as a result, why does he still need to pay tithe since he would have already been justified? Since we that are justified are not expected to pay tithe, why should Abraham's case be any different? It does not make any sense if you think about it.

"…So then they which are of faith are blessed with faithful Abraham" **(Galatians 3:9). (KJV)** (My emphasis). Because we are of faith. God ensured we are yoked together with faithful Abraham, since he is the father of faith; and we are his children. Thus, we claim the same blessings given to Abraham. But the only difference is that it is no longer through Melchizedek, but through The High Priest Himself, Jesus Christ. Whose foreshadow and glimpse God revealed to Abraham in the form of Melchizedek.

"…For as many as are of the works of the law are under the curse: for it is written, Cursed is everyone that continueth not in all things which are written in the book of the law to do them." **(Galatians 3:10)**. (My emphasis). The curse of the law is that everyone that is under the law, must observe hundred percent of what the law required. If the person should observe ninety nine point nine out of a hundred percent, it is not accepted. But with Grace, one can get away with pretty much everything, except the blasphemy against the Holy Spirit; due to the abundance of God's mercy in Jesus Christ. "…So I tell you, every sin and blasphemy can be forgiven-except blasphemy against the Holy Spirit, which will never be forgiven. Anyone who speaks against the Son of Man can be forgiven, but anyone who speaks against the Holy Spirit will never be forgiven, either in this world or in the world to come." **(Matthew 12:31-32) (NLT)**. But Apostle Paul would go on to discourage us not to continue in sin, so Grace can abound. However, this generation of God's children has never been under the law at any time.

Just as we are not under the law, so was Abraham not under the law at the time he gave tithe to Melchizedek. Abraham was governed by the law of faith, not the law of Moses that governed the Israelites. It would take about four hundred and fifty years later after the Israelites left Egypt that the law was given by Moses. Therefore, the issue of tithe supersedes the law. God instilled it in the heart of Abraham to do it, so the children of grace being us can learn from his footsteps and do likewise. Here is my thought. Tithing was ordained because of us, not even because of the Levites but God the all-knowing Father added it to the lists of the different tithes and offerings given to the Levites, to ensure we do not lose track of it until we come to the time appointed.

"…But that no man is justified by the law in the sight of God, it is evident: for, The Just shall live by faith. And the law is not of faith: but, The man that doeth them shall live in them" **(Galatians 3:11-12)**. (My emphasis). So it is clear and evident here that the law and faith are two distinct things of which faith is greater. But yet, we see that God did not credit the law to Abraham, but He credited faith to him instead, just as He is not asking us to live by the law today but by faith. No man is justified in the sight of God by the law, but God justified Abraham by faith and Abraham gave the tithe of all. Again, I ask, why should our case be any different? This is why we may be asked on that day the same question in Malachi three, "Will a man rob God?" And we may not have an answer to give.

Chapter six: The word of God stands forever

"Heaven and earth shall pass away, but my word shall not pass away" (**Matthew chapter 24:35**) **(KJV)**

At what point does the word of God stops being active? At what point does it cease to be effective, viable, potent, effective or relevant? Not at any time. The word of God is forever constant and forever settled in heaven.

"Forever, O Lord, thy word is settled in heaven" (**Psalms chapter 119:89**) **(KJV)** Listen to this;

"God is not a man that He should lie; neither the son of man that He should repent" (**Numbers chapter 23:19**)

"Jesus Christ the same yesterday, and today, and forever" (**Hebrews chapter 13:8**)

People sometimes read God's word and address it in past tense. As if that is where it belong; but this is a bad practice. God's word does not only address the past; it also addresses both the present and the future. This is because…,

"The word of God is quick, and powerful, and sharper than any two-edged sword, piercing even to the dividing asunder of soul and spirit, and of the joints and marrow, and is a discerner of the thoughts and intents of the heart. Neither is there any creature that is not manifest in his sight: but all things are naked and opened unto the eyes of whom we have to do" (**Hebrews chapter 4:12-13**). (My emphasis)

If I am to disobey any of God's word deliberately, it will not be the passage where He spoke with anger and warning and called those disobedient to His command, robbers. No! I would look for another passage instead. It baffles me as to why some people tempt God, including some Christians who ought to know better? I will quickly make this point that the tithe God has asked us to pay is not for anything else; instead, it is for the advancement of His kingdom here earth. How can the kingdom of God advance if there is no money to do the basic things such as having enough food at the storehouse to feed the hungry and the poor? Or pay for the place of worship, which is where people go to, to seek God's face whilst interceding for the nations of the world?

God does not need to come and announce the issue of tithe all over in the New Testament. Just like He does not need to re-announce any of the moral doctrines He laid down in the Old Testament all over in the New Testament, when He already made it clear in the Old Testament. He made His mind clear in the book of Malachi what the indictment is against His children. And funny enough, He did not say, continue to bring in all the tithe into my storehouse until my son comes and delivers you from the curse of this heavy law I have placed upon you before you can stop. Then at-least nobody would be mentioning anything about tithe today. The Bible says in **Psalms chapter 62:11**

"Once have you spoken, twice have I heard that power belongs to God."

This verse implies that God only speaks once to His children, and they should adhere to whatever He says.

John chapter 10:27 "My sheep hear my voice, and I know them, and they follow me."

Numbers chapter 23:19 reads, "God is not the son of man that He should repent." **(KJV)** New Living Translation puts it this way; "God is not a man, so he does not lie. He is not human, so he does not change his mind. Has he ever promised and failed to act? Has he ever promised and not carried it through?"

Psalms chapter 12:6 says; "The words of the Lord are pure words: as silver tried in a furnace of earth, purified seven times."

If these passages are not enough for the believer, here's **Proverbs chapter 30:5;** it says, "Every word of God is pure: he is a shield unto them that put their trust in him."

Psalms chapter 18:30 says; "As for God, his way is perfect: the word of the Lord is tried: He is a buckler to all those that trust in him."

2 Timothy chapter 3:16-17 "All scripture is given by inspiration of God, and is profitable for doctrine, for reproof, for correction, for instruction in righteousness; That the man of God may be perfect, thoroughly furnished unto all good works." So you see my brothers and sisters, God's word is complete, and we use scriptures to interpret and complement scriptures which is what the aim of this book is about. To give you a basic understanding of the nature of the God we serve, before we proceed to the issue of tithing itself.

Chapter seven: How it all began and what the purpose is for

"It is God that works in you both to will and to do his good pleasure" (**Philippians chapter 2:12-15**)

The first time the Bible mentioned tithe was in **Genesis chapter 14:16-20** after Abram returned from defeating *Chedorlaomer* king of Elam, that Melchizedek welcomed him with bread and wine; and blessed him. And Abram's response to God's blessings and protection was to give a tenth of all his plunder. The question is, who laid it on his heart to give a tenth of all he returned with? The answer is God.

Philippians chapter 2:13 says it is God who works in us both to will and to do his good pleasure. Therefore, we can learn from this passage that Abram did not give the tithe because he wanted to, or because he reasoned it was the right thing to do. But because he got prompted to do so by the God that knew the end of a thing before its beginning. The God who fore-knew what the needs of His Church would be many years to come. This would result from the future plans to give provision to the men that would dedicate their lives in service to Him; to the maintenance of the place of worship and of feeding the poor. And in serving Him, they would have no grudge whatsoever or any reason to complain or murmur that they dedicated their entire life to serving the God that does not feed them nor provide for their basic necessities.

This was the case with the Levites during the Old Testament, and for His Church during this dispensation of grace, of the New Testament. He provided to sustain the Levites in their carnality, how much more would He not provide to sustain His Church which is spiritual? He sustained the old covenant with tithes and offering, how do we suggest He sustain the new covenant, His Church and Bride? By throwing money down from the sky so His children can use to pay the Church bills? No, He will not do so because He already laid the foundation. Thus, God laid the first block upon which every other block would be based upon, in His friend, Abraham.

Romans chapter 4:12 "... And the father of circumcision to them who are not of the circumcision only, but who also walk in the steps of that faith of our father Abraham, which he had being yet uncircumcised."

Moving on from Abraham, God instilled it in the heart of Jacob to vow to give a tenth of all that God would give him, back to God; the one that gave all to him in the first place.

Genesis chapter 28:20-22 "If God would be with me, and would keep me in this way that I go, and would give me bread to eat, and raiment to put on. So that I come again to my Father's house in peace: then shall the Lord be my God: and this stone, which I have set for a pillar, shall be God's house: and of all that thou shalt give me I would surely give the tenth unto thee." **(KJV)**

Now let's have a look at the basis of Jacob's vow. First he said, "If God would be with me, and would keep me in this way that I go, and would give me bread to eat, and raiment to put on. So that I come again to my Father's house in peace, then I will..." Has God been with us? Has He kept us in all our ways and rebuked the enemy for our sake? Gave us bread to eat, or has He left us to die in hunger?

"I have been young, and now am old, yet have I not seen the righteous forsaken, nor his seed begging bread" **(Psalms chapter 37:25). (KJV)**

Has He put clothes on us or left us to go in rags? Has He gone with us during all those times we travelled, and brought us back home in peace, or did He left us to perish by the arrows that flies at noonday?

"It is of the Lord's mercies that we are not consumed because his compassion fail not. They are new every morning, great is thy faithfulness" (**Lamentations chapter 3:22-23**). **(KJV)** (My emphasis), If men of the Old Testament were able to honour God with tithes because God kept them, why should we of the New Testament not give tithe? If not for anything else, to recognise God's faithfulness and Lordship over our lives?

Now to fast-forward to the time of the Levitical priesthood in **Leviticus 27:30-34.** Just in-case the children of Israel failed to understand the importance and implications of what both Abraham and Jacob did, God ensured it becomes binding by making it a command every one of them should obey; though they would later refuse to obey, the same way some of us are refusing to obey today. Brethren this command is still binding today whether we chose to identify with it or distance ourselves. I cannot recall reading from any passage in the Bible where God said sorry guys, these commandments are no-longer applicable because my Son paid the price. In fact, the price Jesus paid was the price for sin, and the tithe they were commanded to pay was not for their sins to be forgiven, but for the work of God to continue.

The price Jesus paid is not so people can ignore the law and become

51

lawbreakers. No! He paid it, so that when we do any good works (acts of righteousness), our works can be accepted before God. This was not the case in the time past when all our works (acts of righteousness) were counted as filthy rag before God. The question now is, whose report would you believe? Would you believe the lies the enemy instilled in people's minds and mouths, so they can disobey God as he himself did, or will you believe the report of the Lord? And by the way, is ten per cent such a significant amount that we feel is too big to give back to the One that gave us life and sustained us daily, including our families? If we truly believe our Lord Jesus Christ gave his life for us, is giving ten per cent of our income too much to give so his work here on earth can advance? No, ten percent is an insignificant amount compared to what the Lord has done for us!

Chapter eight: The case of the alabaster box of ointment

There is a story in the book of **Luke chapter 7:36-50.** A Pharisee named Simon invited Jesus for a meal. Shortly after Jesus arrived at his house, a woman came in with an alabaster box, filled with ointment and began to wash Jesus's feet with her tears. After washing his feet, she kissed and dried them with her hair and anointed them with oil. After observing the events as they unfold, Simon said within himself, indeed, if this man is truly a prophet, he would have known what kind of person this woman is, a sinner. Jesus knowing his heart, (after telling him a story of two debtors who owed their creditor. One owing five hundred pence and the other fifty. And when they were unable to pay back their debts, their creditor forgave them both) asked him, "Which of these two men would love their creditor, who forgave them, the most?" And Simon replied, the one forgiving most, which owed five hundred pence. Jesus; after opening his eyes, by giving him a lecture of all the things that woman did, said to Simon, "... Wherefore, I say unto thee, her sins, which are many, are forgiven; for she loved much: but

to whom little is forgiven, the same
loved little."

Now, with this story in hindsight,
between the people of the Old Testament
and those of the New Testament; between
the dispensation of the Law and the
dispensation of Grace; which of these
two, fall into any of the two
categories of debtors mentioned by
Jesus, above? It is obvious the New
Testament believers fall within the
category of that sinful woman that
demonstrated how much sin had been
forgiven her.

She would not only break her bank
to anoint the feet which brought this
Gospel of Peace and Forgiveness to her,
but would go as far as washing Jesus's
feet with her tears and drying them
with her hair and kisses. This would
demonstrate selflessness and great
humility. A great lesson for us the
children of this dispensation of Grace
to emulate from. The Bible says in
Romans Chapter 15:4 that everything
has been written for our learning. If
that is true, then wisdom demands that
we put whatever good things we learn
into practice. We can learn from this
woman to not hoard the things we
treasure the most in life especially
money, more than God, but to surrender
them for the use of our Lord and
Saviour.

Everything we do or asked to do as Christians are in response to faith, love, grace, and to unmerited favour. Just like Jacob did. It was grace that Jacob went out empty and returned full with treasures. It was through faith he vowed to give tithe if God would be with him during his sojourn. It was the love of God that kept him alive when his father-in-law would have dealt with him severely, for having sneaked away without him knowing. And it was through God's unmerited favour that his life was preserved when he encountered his brother Esau on his way back; when he would have paid so dearly with his life for swindling his brother out of his blessings, but yet lived to tell the story.

Chapter nine: Reason For The Tithe

"And behold, I have given the children of Levi all the tenth in Israel for an inheritance, for their service which they serve, even the service of the tabernacle of the congregation. Neither must the children of Israel henceforth come nigh the tabernacle of the congregation, lest they bear sin, and die. But the Levites shall do the service of the tabernacle of the congregation, and they shall bear their iniquity: **it shall be a statute forever throughout your generations**, that among the children of Israel they have no inheritance. But the tithes of the children of Israel, which they offer as an heave offering unto the Lord, I have given to the Levites to inherit: therefore, I have said unto them, among the children of Israel they shall have no inheritance" **(Numbers 18:21-26) (KJV)**

(My emphasis) God desired Priests that would do His bidding amongst the people. He desired those that would be dedicated to His service and errands, He chose the Levites. And because the labourer is worthy of his hire, according to **Luke chapter 10:7**, He gave them the tithes that belonged to Him as their reward.

One thing to mention before moving forward is this, the tithes of the people do not belong to the Priests or anybody else; they belong to God. The One who owns the universe and everything that is in it, according to **Psalms 24:1.** God's will on tithing is, "I want every ten percent of your income or profit." And what I do with it is my business, not yours to judge.

Matthew chapter 20:15 "Is it not lawful for me to do what I will with mine own? Is thine eye evil, because I am good?" (KJV)

The problem with some of us is that we are trying to dictate to God. Not only are we trying to dictate to Him, we are also judging Him that He has no right to demand the ten percent of our income because we think it is too much to give to Him. This is the problem some of us are having with God. Just like Judas Iscariot, when he saw how much oil Mary (the sister of Martha & Lazarus) supposedly wasted just to anoint the feet of Jesus in **John chapter 12:5** asked, "Why was not this ointment sold for three hundred pence, and given to the poor?"

He questioned people's generosity towards God, and also God's willingness to accept such huge generosity from the people, instead of giving them to the poor. Today, many people are saying, I would rather give the money to the poor, instead of these Pastors. But what they fail to understand is that whatever belongs to God must be given to God. He alone decides what He intends to use it for. Besides, there are portions for the poor. If we decide to give God's portion to the poor, what happens to the portion we are commanded to give to the poor, alongside our tithes? What happens to it? You see, this is where the robbing starts from.

In the argument with my Sunday school teacher, I tried to come up with good reasons as to why it would be a better idea to rather give my ten percent to the needy, instead of giving them to God. I carefully came up with a very good scenario that would justify my actions not to give tithes to God, and this is what the enemy does on a daily basis to people, to provide them with valid reasons to disobey the voice of God. Who am I to change God's original order of things? But here's the truth: the analogy I gave about the man whose wife was sick and needed to be taken to the hospital, even if it was a true story; the truth still remains that it would have been a one-off incident. Thus, if I should use a one-off incident to justify my perpetual disobedience to God, what happens after wards with my subsequent tithes? Obviously, I would have used a one-off scenario to justify my actions to rob God. Here's the bad news: the

Almighty knows all about our little depraved minds and thoughts, because His foolishness is wiser than man's wisdom. As far as God is concerned, the ordinance of tithing is forever.

Chapter ten: Will a man rob God?

Not too long ago, there was an uproar, about a trending news on social media. A popular man of God, Pastor E.A Adeboye made a statement and said: "Anyone not paying his tithe isn't making it to Heaven"!

When I first heard this statement, I was furious and angry as to why such great man of God, respected by many, should bring himself so low? How dare he make such statement? No wonder some people have lost all respect for God and for His Church? After pondering on the matter, I came to the conclusion: anyone making such comment had either lost their senses or had no clue what great work Jesus did on the cross. How on earth can he make such statement? He of all people should have been able to know salvation is free, through the precious blood of our Lord Jesus, and not because of one's tithe. However, let us dig a bit deeper and find out if this man of God is right or wrong.

"Will a man rob God? Yet ye have robbed me. But ye say, wherein have we robbed thee? In tithes and offerings." **(Malachi chapter 3:8)(KJV)**

Malachi chapter 3:8 is one of the most astonishing statements of accusation ever made by God against the children of Israel. And whether this statement is applicable to us today or not, is not important at this stage. For now, let us consider His Words carefully from Malachi 3:1

"Behold, I will send my messenger, and he shall prepare the way before me: and the Lord, whom ye seek, shall suddenly come to His temple, even the messenger of the covenant, whom ye delight in: behold, he shall come, saith the Lord of hosts" (**Malachi chapter 3:1**). (My emphasis) First we need to acknowledge that the book of Malachi is the last book of the Old Testament. Not only that, the very last two chapters are directly linked to the New Testament and the Messiah. I believe the book of Malachi is linked to the New Testament because, it contains the immediate future plans regarding what God purposed to do. Some may argue, just because it is the last book of the Old Testament doesn't necessarily mean it is the nearest to the New Testament, but let us ignore this factor for the time being. The book of Malachi is a concatenation of the two Testaments, which weaved the two Testaments together, just as the word of God is interwoven and cannot be separated, irrespective of how hard we try to separate it.

Therefore, in this passage, the Lord was unequivocally clear He would be sending His messenger to prepare the way of the Lord, whom the children of

Israel longed after, at the time. And the messenger He would be sending is the man we know as John the Baptist, who did prepare the way for our Lord Jesus. Jesus Himself confirmed it by saying this concerning John, "For this is he, of whom it is written, Behold, I send my messenger before thy face, which shall prepare the way before thee." (**Matthew chapter 11:10**).

The book of Malachi is as important as the entire New Testament. For without it, and other books of the Old Testament which prophesied about the coming of our Lord Jesus Christ, we would be lost, with no clue who Jesus is, or the things that point to Him. So, it is important to acknowledge every detail of this book and pay close attention to what the Father is saying in it.

"But who may abide the day of his coming? And who shall stand when He appears? For He is like a refiner's fire, and like fuller's soap: And He shall sit as a refiner and purifier of silver: and He shall purify the sons of Levi. And purge them as gold and silver. That they may offer unto the Lord an offering in righteousness" (**Malachi chapter 3:2-3**)

This passage not only foretold of the first coming of Jesus, but also gave a glimpse of His second coming when no man would be able to stand in

His presence. The day He will sit as a Refiner and Judge of all, to separate the wheat from the chaff. **Matthew chapter 25:31-32** says, "When the Son of man shall come in his glory, and all the holy angels with Him, then shall he sit upon the throne of His glory: And before Him shall be gathered all nations: and he shall separate them one from another, as a shepherd divideth his sheep from the goats." In reading the book of Malachi, one cannot mistake what was important to God and what He was about to do. In saying this, I am inferring that everything in the entire chapter three of the book of Malachi were events channelled to the future, as opposed to past events. Let me re-emphasise, the book of Malachi chapter three were events linked to the future, not with the past. Therefore, it would be absurd for anyone after reading, to separate the words spoken in them, by assigning some with the past and some with the future. All belongs to the future.

Now, let me start by asking this question: why was it the sons of Levi He was coming to purify? Why not the sons of Jacob or the sons of Abraham as a whole? The answer is simple: the Levites were all Priests. They were the ones tasked the duty of offering gifts and sacrifices to the Almighty God. It was their office and duty to offer gifts and sacrifices to the Lord forever. But what does it matter anyway? It matters because He was drawing a correlation between the Levites and the Church or new kingdom He was about to build. The kingdom which would comprise mainly of Priests, according to **1 Peter chapter 2:9**. A kingdom or Church whereby everyone would have the ability to offer gifts and sacrifices themselves without the involvement of a middleman.

But hang on a minute, why would He still require them to offer gifts and sacrifices after that the Lord, whom they seek, would have come and purified them? It does not make sense if He would still be willing and waiting for those already purified to continue in their duty of sacrifice, and gift rendition after having already been purified; according to those who argue we should not pay tithe? The answer is simple: the coming of the Messiah does not signify the end of offering sacrifices and gifts to God, rather, so the gifts can be more acceptable by God, now that they had been cleansed and purified.

"Then shall the offering of Judah and Jerusalem be pleasant unto the Lord, as in the days of old, and as the former years" (**Malachi chapter 3:4**)

As mentioned above, part of the work Jesus came to do was to make the

64

offerings of God's people pleasant, and acceptable before God. In other words, His coming was not intended to stop God's people bringing their offerings or tithes unto Him. Instead, it was so that when they do, the offerings and tithes will be pleasant and acceptable before God. Not just their offerings or tithes, but also their deeds, actions, renditions, worship, praise, meditations and sacrifices. It is only and after our sins are forgiven that our offerings and sacrifices can be accepted. Which is why Christ died so our sins can be forgiven and our sacrifices made acceptable.

Matthew chapter 5:23-24 states, "Therefore, if thou bring thy gift to the altar, and there, remember that thy brother hath aught against thee: leave there thy gift before the altar, and go thy way: first be reconciled to thy brother, and then come and offer thy gift." You see, only when the first is done can the second be done successfully. Our offerings and gifts cannot be accepted if we bring them covered with sin. God is not desperate for offerings and gifts or tithes, though He commands us to bring them. It is a waste of time and personal resources when we think we can bribe God with our offerings whilst living in sin, because they will never be accepted by God. The person might as well use whatever gift they came with to do something else instead of wasting them, thinking God is pleased with them. This is where some Ministers of God get it wrong. They know vividly that the people are living in sin; instead of warning them to repent, they pretend they know nothing. This is undoubtedly because they know that should they address the situation, there is the fear that such people would stop coming to their church and, if that happens, the offerings and tithes they bring would equally stop, thereby depriving some of them of their ostentatious lifestyles they are used to.

"For I am the LORD, I change not: therefore, ye sons of Jacob are not consumed" **(Malachi chapter 3:6)**. Before the Lord would go on to bring an indictment against the children of Israel, He first assured them of who He Is: that He does not change, as many today unwisely think He does. He is always constant. He has not changed as a result of the time intervals between His Word. If He does change, none of us would be alive today and that will not mean His enemy would destroy us, no! He Himself would have destroyed us all. So He does not change, and we are grateful He does not.

Today people are so clever, thinking they can out-smart God by using the New Testament as a tool to exclude themselves from obeying the word of God, saying God has changed from what He had previously said. God has not, and will never change.

They say, 'thus says the Lord' when the Lord has not spoken. Nowhere in the New Testament did God say we are not to pay tithes. Therefore, if He never said so, why do we assume He did? It is a big error of judgment. I have read the Bible and I am yet to come across a passage where it says I am no longer required to pay my tithes because Christ has paid all on the Cross. If that is the case, why only tithes? Why not offerings as well? Because they both took root from the Old Testament. So, God does not change and His Word stands forever. I want you to underline these words as we continue, because this is the word that settles all the arguments about tithing. From the time and day the Lord made this statement to a billion years to come, He will still stand on His Word, and we can bet our lives on it. He said, "I am the Lord, I change not!" Brethren, this is an emphatic statement. If the Lord does not change, His Words too cannot change. There is no better way to say it. We are not talking about the law and its requirements here. Instead, we're talking about His 'eternal Word.' We are talking about the sure statements He uttered with everything that made Him who He is. The Bible says in **Psalms chapter 138:2** "... For thou has magnified thy word above all thy names." Why? Because, the word of God is infallible, and free from any form of error; thus, cannot be altered, changed, modified, replaced or updated with time. Why? Because "God is not a man that He should lie, neither the son of man that He should repent: hath He said, and shall He not do it? Or hath He spoken, and shall He not make it good?" (**Numbers chapter 23:19**). The reason God magnified His Word above all His Names is so His creation can continually bank on everything He says without any shadow of doubt. It is so that mankind can trust in Him, and lean on everything which proceeds out of His mouth.

"Even from the days of your fathers ye are gone away from mine ordinances, and have not kept them. Return unto me, and I'll return unto thee, saith the Lord of hosts. But you said, wherein shall we return?" (**Malachi chapter 3:7**)

(My emphasis) This statement is a future statement as though God is in the future asking His people to return to Him, and they are asking, wherein shall we return? And He said, you have gone away from mine ordinances, right from the days of your fathers. This leaves one to wonder, when were the days of our fathers? Were they not the days of the Mosaic Laws, when they lived by the laws, and during the days of the Levitical Priesthood? Thus, God is speaking in the present that we have forsaken His ordinances like we did in the days of our fathers and that we should return unto Him in the new era He is establishing. It is a sad thing if and when unbelievers are asking, "Wherein shall we return?" the same question some believers of today still equally ask. Any wonder the world is in chaos today? No wonder many believers are now blackmailing God, querying and making excuses with everything He says, in the name of grace.

"Will a man rob God? Yet ye have robbed me. But ye say, wherein have we robbed thee? In tithes and offerings? Ye are cursed with a curse: for ye have robbed me, even this whole nation" **(Malachi chapter 3:8-9)**

(My emphasis). Let me begin by saying this: forget about what any pastor has ever said to you regarding the issue of tithe. Forget about what the critics of the Bible have ever said about tithes. Forget about what all the self-ordained men and women of God on the internet have ever said about tithes. You, as an intellectual, learned and intelligent being, who claim to be a child of God; filled with the Holy Spirit; what do you make about this statement? "Will a man rob God?" What answer does your heart give to you when you read this passage? It is important to note that on the last day none of these categories of people mentioned above will stand by to defend you when you stand before the Throne, to be judged by the Almighty God. Or, do you not know that every man will be judged at the last day according to their deeds? If this particular verse of the scripture stands to accuse you on that day, what defence or excuse will you give? What did the Bible say in **2 Timothy chapter 3:16-17**? It reads... "All Scripture is given by inspiration of God, and is profitable for doctrine, for reproof, for correction, for instruction in righteousness, that the man of God may be perfect, thoroughly furnished unto all good works." This passage is emphatically clear that the entire Scripture or Bible as we call it, are inspired by God and it is the totality of God's counsel for His children. Why? Because it is 'profitable' amongst many other things, for doctrine.

So, let me ask you again, what is your defence against the above statement that asks, will a man rob God? I want to believe that the subject of tithing is very important to God for Him to equate those who are non-compliant to robbers. And He will be unjust to label the people of the Old Testament robbers for not complying with tithing and yet excuse us when we replicate the same thing they did. And far be it from God to be unjust. Far be it from God that what He once called sin, He would now accept and call righteousness because of our way of thinking.

And, on that note, here is my conclusion about this matter, and I am being as objective as I can possibly be, not as a result of what Pastor E.A Adeboye said, but based on the evidences from the Bible. If the Word of God is true which it is, no robber will make it to Heaven. How? Because according to the Bible, which says, "Know ye not that the unrighteous shall not inherit the Kingdom of God? Be not deceived: neither fornicators, nor idolaters, nor adulterers, nor effeminate, nor abusers of themselves with mankind, nor thieves, nor covetous, nor drunkards, nor revellers, nor extortioners, shall inherit the kingdom of God" (**1 Corinthians chapter 6:9-10**). (KJV)

Brethren, this is the New Testament speaking. It did not say these categories of people mentioned above will not inherit the Kingdom of God if they are living under the Law, or if they are living under Grace. The time dispensation is inconsequential because God is God, and His standard is righteousness and truth. He is the same yesterday, today and forever (**Hebrews 13:8**). No, it is not possible for a man to rob God!

So you see, anybody that claims to be a Christian and yet deliberately chooses to disobey any part of God's word, not just tithing, will not make Heaven, due to their lack of reverence to God's words. Not because tithe is greater than the work Jesus did on the cross, but because it is a direct disobedience to the Word of God. One thing about robbers is that they know what they intend to do before going ahead to actually doing it. God did not say these people are thieves, which would have been a trivial case. But He said they are robbers which makes it more serious.

Robbers are those that will not hesitate to kill and destroy in other to get away with what belongs to others. But robbing God in this context is to device every means possible, so as to get away with what rightfully belongs to God. Thus, my argument is, if God would make such a strong statement against non-tithers in the Old Testament, why would He, on the spur-of-the-moment, repent and not call them robbers just a few years down the line? The reason He will not repent is because if He does, every other sin would be permissible, and we would not need worry about the consequences of living a careless life or living an immoral life style. You judge for yourself.

If the Old Testament law condemns a man for stealing, and calls Him a thief, why do you think the dispensation of Grace will justify the same person just because Christ died on the cross? Again, has God changed? A thief is a thief. The best a thief can do is to repent and stop stealing, so he can be forgiven instead of justifying his actions in the name of Grace. Otherwise, both murderers, fornicators, adulterers, liars and all the rest can as well continue in their sinful ways and justify their actions in the name of "Dispensation of Grace," you judge for yourself.

Now if the foregoing did not convince you about tithing, let us have a look at one more scripture before proceeding: "Now the works of the flesh are manifest, which are these, Adultery, fornication, uncleanness, lasciviousness, idolatry, witchcraft, hatred, variance, emulations, wrath, strife, seditions, heresies, envyings, murders, drunkenness, revellings, and such like: of the which I tell you before, as I have also told you in time past, that they which do such things shall not inherit the kingdom of God" **(Galatians chapter 5:19-21) (KJV)**

Let us consider the categories of people listed in the above passage once again, which the Bible categorically says shall not inherit the kingdom of God. These categories of people will not inherit the kingdom of God whether they are supposedly born again or not. Whether they are living under the dispensation of the Law of Moses, or under the dispensation of Grace makes no difference. And this does not mean the finished work of Jesus isn't powerful enough to save them, but as a result of their decision to remain as they are, instead of allowing the Lord to transform them through the finished work. One of the words mentioned is the word 'heresy.' I would like to welcome all those that preach against tithing to take a moment and reflect on the above passage and meaning of this word. The word 'heresy', according to the dictionary, is defined as 'a belief or action that most people think is wrong, because it disagrees with beliefs that are generally accepted.'

The synonyms for the word heresy are: "unorthodox, apostasy, dissidence," and many more. These words are very strong words if used to describe a person, let alone a Christian. Do you know that these are the words the Bible warned us against? The state of apostasy is a state of no return and any Christian that can be described as such should better make hay while the sun shines. Those who practice heresies are called heretics. Who can be called a heretic? A heretic is anybody, (especially a religious person) that has a contrary belief to what the majority of the people are used to and held dear. Anybody that strongly disagrees and acts in ways that contravenes the Orthodoxical tenets are called heretics.

Those that are preaching against tithing have no solid Biblical reference to back their disagreements. The only valid reference for them or anyone else would have been anywhere at all our Lord Jesus made a comment that suggests He is not in support of it. That would have been a valid reference and a good reason for us to follow what Jesus said. But in this case, Jesus our Master and Saviour said nothing against tithing. And if He did not say anything against tithing, it would be absurd for Apostle Paul to turn up to the scene a few years later and preach against what Jesus never preached against; that makes no sense at all. Permit me to rephrase the statement: If Jesus, who is superior to Paul (being Paul's own LORD, Master and Saviour as well) did not speak against tithe, why should it be Paul he would give the licence to, to do so? Was he afraid to preach against it when he clearly had the opportunity to do so, or simply because there was not any sense in doing so, since the mind of God is clear, thus leaving Him with one option which was to encourage them to continue on them? **Matthew chapter 23:23**

I believe that all the teachings and preaching of Apostle Paul were inspired from two major sources: the written Word and the revelations of the Holy Spirit. If this was so, I find it hard to believe that God will reveal a contradictory message for him to preach. And Paul never preached any contradictory message either. Everything he preached are consistent with what both Jesus, John the Baptist and the rest of the Apostles preached. And that message is that salvation is a free gift that cannot be earned through hard work or bought with money.

Here is one more thing that does not make sense. The idea that tithe compliance automatically eradicates the finished work of Christ, thereby exposing one back at the mercy of the Law. This is ludicrous! How can it be? When they were still under the Law, they were not required to pay tithe for their sins to be forgiven. In fact, tithe had nothing to do with their sin been forgiven or not forgiven. Rather, it was a sacrificial lamb the sinner brings to atone for his or her sins. It would have made sense if the reverse was the case, that any sinner that brought their tithes gets their sins cancelled under the law, that would have been a perfect case as it would be evident for all that no more tithe paying for debt of sin because we now have One that freely forgives it without the paying of tithe.

Now, there was an event that led to
Paul rebuking the Church in Galatia,
in **Galatians chapter 3**. The event was
not because the people argued about the
legitimacy of tithing. No, the event
was an issue about circumcision which
started from the previous chapter and
boiled over. According to the Law of
Moses, only the Jews are considered
God's chosen people based on the
covenant of circumcision God made with
Abraham; not the covenant of tithing.
And so, it made perfect sense for
Apostle Paul to step in at the time of
conflict and misunderstanding on the
subject, to clarify that in this
dispensation of grace, physical
circumcision or uncircumcision matters
nothing to God. Why? Because, although
the issue of circumcision is the
bedrock of faith in both Testaments.
Yet, there is a difference to the kind
of circumcision now required in the New
Testament. The kind of circumcision we
are required to do is that of the
heart, as opposed to the flesh. All
this started with Apostle Peter's
attitude towards some of the brethren
who were uncircumcised, in which he
distanced himself, fearing those that
were circumcised would revolt, should
they see him eating and drinking with
those considered uncircumcised. His
actions were such that had the
potential to divide the early church.
That even Barnabas, though considered
matured, almost got carried away had
Paul not stepped in. It was not because

they did argue about whether to pay or not to pay tithe? It would have been a different thing should it had been the reason Paul was rebuking them: On the contrary. I want to believe that, should the incident that happened regarding Apostle Peter's actions not having taken place, there would not had been a need for Paul to rebuke them, and we would not have been having these conversations regarding whether or not we should pay tithes today

Chapter eleven: The things that belong to God and the things that belong to Caesar

"Tell us therefore, what thinkest thou? Is it lawful to give tributes to Caesar, or not? But Jesus perceived their wickedness, and said, why tempt ye me, ye hypocrites? Shew me the tribute money. And they brought unto Him a penny. And he saith unto them, whose is this image and superscription? They say unto Him, Caesar's. Then saith he unto them, render therefore unto Caesar the things which are Caesar's, and unto God the things that are God's." **(Matthew chapter 22:17-21) (KJV)**

One of the things the Jews and Pharisees looked for to use as a trap against Jesus was to catch Him say anything contradictory to the law. Something as a proof he was breaking the law, so they can stone Him to death, and give justification for their actions. So they asked Him, sir, with all due respect, "Is it lawful to pay tributes (taxes) to Caesar?" And Jesus after showing them the superscription on the money which had the head of Caesar on it, told them to render to Caesar what belongs to Caesar and to God, what belongs to God. On hearing this, they all left Him alone because his answer gave no indication He was a law breaker.

Here are the things we can learn from this story: there are things which duly belong to Caesar, and things that rightfully belong to God. And just in case one might be wondering who Caesar is, the 'Caesar' in our time is the government. Every time we buy, sell, work or do any form of business that yields dividend, we are obliged to pay tax towards it. This is one of the many ways governments bring in revenues, and anybody who refuses to pay tax becomes a law breaker, and at the mercy of the government who would go the distance to ensure every penny is recovered: as well as imposed fines in addition. So let me ask you who said we should not pay tithe, do you pay taxes? If you do, why? Is it because you fear the government or because you have no choice? It is obvious you are not afraid of the government, I'm guessing. The reason you pay this tax is because you have no choice. If you did, you would not pay it just like some people will try as much as they can to dodge the paying of taxes.

Now let's come to that of God. What are the things that belong to God? Oh yes! There are things God laid claim of in the Bible and any good Bible student should be able to pick a few of those things. For example, **Psalms chapter 24:1** states, "The earth is the Lord's, and the fullness thereof, the world and they that dwell in it."

The entire world we live in belongs to God, including the people, you and me, and all the other resources in the world: all belongs to God. The next example so not to bore you is the tithe.

Leviticus chapter 27:30 states, "And all the tithe of the land, whether of the seed of the land, or of the fruit of the tree, is the Lord's: it is holy unto the Lord."

The Lord Himself told His people that all the tithes of the land belongs to Him. The reason He called non-compliers robbers in the book of Malachi, is because they refused to pay it. They withheld what the Lord Himself consecrated and called "holy", unto Himself. So let me ask again, you who refuse to pay your tithe as a Christian, what are your reasons? Is it because you are not afraid of God, or because you think you have a choice to pay or not to pay? I pray these two questions do not come back to haunt us at the end.

I want to believe the main reason people are now refusing to pay their tithes is because they think they have a choice. Not necessarily because they claim its part of the law that was abolished by Jesus. Unlike what belongs to Caesar which they have no choice because Caesar would definitely come for them, whereas, God would not come for them the same way Caesar would. How can we justify ourselves in this matter? The same Jesus, who rebuked his disciples in **Luke chapter 6:46** by asking,

"…And why call ye me, Lord, Lord, and do not the things which I say?"

Is the same Jesus that say we should give to Caesar what belongs to Caesar and to God what belongs to God. Why do we infer our Lord Jesus said what he did not say? Why do we add to the Scripture what is not in the Scripture? There are things that deservedly belong to God, if not, Jesus would not ask them to give to God what belongs to God. So, what are the things that belongs to God?

Those that argue we should not pay tithe should present a passage from the scripture, where our Lord Jesus said we should not pay tithes or where the Apostles said we should not pay tithes. We cannot find anywhere in the entire Bible where such statement was made. However, what you will see are passages that complement other passages in agreement to what has already been said, not in contradiction because the Word of God does not contradict itself, which is what people imply when they say the new dispensation Christians should distance themselves from anything that has to do with the law and tithing.

Chapter twelve: Why pray, fast and give alms, as New Testament believers?

"Take heed that ye do not your alms before men, to be seen of them: otherwise ye have no reward of your Father which is in Heaven..." **(Matthew chapter 6:1-18)(KJV)**

In this passage, Jesus explained to his audience the right way to give alms, the right way to pray and fast, which leaves one to wonder: where did He get these doctrines from? Was it him who instituted them, or did he take them from the Book of the Law? Why is it a good thing for us to pray, since Jesus who is our High Priest, is even seated at the right hand of God interceding for us? Why do we fast, when it is not Jesus that instructed us to? Why do we give alms, since it was not Jesus that initially ordain the idea of alms-giving? Were these doctrines not from the Law? Why do we continue in them today? If Jesus had done away with everything that has to do with the law, surely we are not supposed to do any of these things, as the logic should go.

So let me ask those who make the arguments that Christians ought not to pay tithes: do you fast and pray? What about the giving of alms? If you answer yes to any of them, can you explain the reason you think they (which are towards man) are very important to your journey as a Christian but the tithe (which is given directly to God) is not

Chapter thirteen: The dangers of wrong assumptions

"Anyone with ears to hear must listen to the Spirit and understand what he is saying to the churches. Write this letter to the angel of the church in Laodicea. This is the message from the one who is the Amen-the faithful and true witness, the beginning of God's new creation: I know all the things you do, that you are neither hot nor cold. I wish that you were one or the other! But since you are like lukewarm water, neither hot nor cold, I will spit you out of my mouth! You say, 'I am rich. I have everything I want. I don't need a thing!' and you don't realize that you are wretched and miserable and poor and blind and naked" **(Revelation chapter 3:13-17) (NLT)**

Which church is the Laodicean church and where is it located geographically? Do you realise that all seven churches mentioned in Revelation pre-existed in the past, in the 'now and the future?' These churches also represent the different phases and eras; the different forms of understandings of the doctrines of our Lord Jesus Christ: the different revelations, interpretations and relationship between God's children with the Gospel of our Lord Jesus Christ. You see, every Church denomination in our time and after our time fall within one of the seven classes of churches already mentioned, as a reference point for us in checkmating our spiritual lives. What are the issues found with the Laodicean church?

The fault our Lord Jesus found with the Laodicean church is this; they said they are rich, they increased with goods and in need of nothing. Basically they said we have everything; and need do nothing. We will be greatly blessed, if we take some moment in asking the Holy Spirit to explain what this verses is talking about? How can a church say "I am rich?" Rich with What? How can a church say "I am increased with goods?" What goods? How can a church say "I have need of nothing?" What nothing? Are these verses in anyway referring to material goods or possession? No! it is not talking about material riches but spiritual riches; and the voices sounded exactly familiar with what most people are saying today on how Christ paid the price for us, how he has giving us everything, and we are increased with all the heavenly blessings and how we need not do anything or work, regarding our salvation? How wrong were they? Very wrong; which is why our Lord Jesus had to step in to rebuke them: and he is doing the same today to you that is reading this book for you not to make the same wrong assumptions.

Assumptions with God can be catastrophic as it can cause us to be lukewarm and inconsistent in our relationship with God. It is rather better and safer for our assumptions to steer us towards doing more than we are required to do in terms of good works; than for it to lead us to be labelled as lukewarm, wicked and disobedient servants. May you not come short of what is required of you in Jesus name! Therefore brethren, the arguments about tithing been part of the law can only be as a result of people's assumptions; and this is a wrong assumption. Because, even if tithing is linked with the law, we have not totally escaped the law, we are still yoked with it as we will be discovering later.

Chapter fourteen: God's indictment to robbers

"But we are all as an unclean thing, and all our righteousness are as filthy rags; and we all do fade as a leaf; and our iniquities, like the wind, have taken us away." **(Isaiah 64:6) (KJV)**

All our *righteousness* are as filthy rags before God, and yet, no one can make it to heaven without them. All our dos and don'ts are as filthy rags before God, and yet no one can behold the face of God without them. All our *works* are as filthy rags before God, and yet, we cannot claim to be Christians or believers without them. For He says, be ye holy for I'm holy because without holiness, no man will see God. **(Hebrews chapter 12:14)**

Righteousness, holiness, purity and the rest, though they appear before God as filthy rags does not mean they are filthy rags to the extent we should abandon and stop pursuing after them. They are still acceptable to God though they appear as filthy rags. But what God did is to wash them clean through the blood of Jesus, so they become robe of righteousness. It is Jesus that polishes and shines them to become robe of righteousness.

Without our works, Jesus will have nothing to shine and polish, let alone presenting to God. As the High Priest, he has to carry something to present to God and that thing is our works which in the time past He considered as filthy rags: but now He washed clean with his blood, so they can be acceptable to God. The only way you recognise a true Christian is by the things they do. The same way you identify a non-believer is equally by the things they do or refuse to do. So we cannot escape works no matter how hard we try to reason they are no longer there. No matter how hard we try to get rid of them. Our works are the things which make or break us; though they are not the things that save us, yet without them, we are illegitimate children, or children of the devil. The Bible says it is by their fruits that you will know them. By their actions you will know them and the devil knows this as well. We cannot be Christians without works. Our works are the things that validates us before God as His children.

Tithing is not part of the law from the beginning. It preceded the law; but added in other to be preserved. Abraham gave his tithe to Melchizedek and this happened more than four hundred years before the Law of Moses. This goes to show that tithing is superior to the Law (within this context) because God ordained it upon the foundation of a better promise, faith. Which the Bible would later go on to say that without faith, it is impossible to please God (**Hebrews chapter 11:1**). Abraham being the father of faith or the father of all those who would later on believe. Abraham gave his tithe to the priest of the Most High God. The shadow of Jesus at the time, showing us to whom all tithes should be ascribed unto in due time, and that time is this time of Grace. The book of Hebrews gave us a vivid picture and comparison between Melchizedek and Jesus. When Abraham gave his tithe to Melchizedek, he blessed him with bread and wine; the same thing Jesus would later give to his disciples before his crucifixion. But let us revisit the book of Hebrews chapter seven for more details of what Abraham did many years ago.

"... For this Melchizedek, King of Salem, priest of the most high God, who met Abraham returning from the slaughter of the kings, and blessed him; to whom also Abraham gave a tenth part of all; first being by interpretation King of righteousness, and after that also King of Salem, which is, King of peace;" **(Hebrews chapter 7:1-2) (KJV)**

(My emphasis) Here, we see the writer of the book of Hebrews, going into deeper details and explanations in other for us to catch a glimpse of the magnitude of the person of

90

Melchizedek, whom Abraham gave the tenth of all to. And said, this king of Salem was a priest of the Most High God. Not a priest to men, but his priesthood was unto God Almighty. *(Jesus would later take on this role when he offered his blood, and entered into the holy of holies with his blood, appearing before the Father, mediating between us and the Father)*

He went into further details and said; he was the king of righteousness and peace. The writer of Hebrews wants to get our attention to something and this is very important. Melchizedek, is said to be first the king of peace, and then priest of the Most High God. All these titles belongs to our Lord Jesus Christ. It is important to understand that because the time for our Lord Jesus Christ to be revealed was not due at the time: God sent him in the form of Melchizedek, so he can bless the one he called his friend, Abraham. God did a very symbolic thing here, in the sense that he met Abraham at the point of him returning from the slaughter of kings, signifying that Abraham's victory over those kings was not obtained by his own strength, but by the power of the Most High God. After-all, how many were Abraham's servants whom he used to fight those kings, compared to the thousands of armies he defeated? Thus, the Lord met him at this crucial point and took a tenth of the spoil, a tenth of his profit and a tenth of his strength.

Brethren, the Lord had no need to collect anything from Abraham. Because this Melchizedek is a King as well as Priest after all. He does not need to collect absolutely anything from Abraham, as we all know: every beast of the forest and the cattle upon the thousand hills belongs to Him to start with. (**Psalms chapter 50:10**). Now here is a shocking statement; the Lord did not need the tithe in other for the Levites to live either, He could have allotted them double portion amongst their brethren, so they can have more than enough to do His work: but He established tithe in Abraham, in the manner He did for the people of this generation.

Therefore, if the only reason He introduced tithe was just so the Levites would succeed, He does not need to, all He could have done would have been to give them their own portion or even go as far as doubling it if need be. But no, His plan is to link Abraham directly to us in this new dispensation as mentioned above, so we can have a reference point.

"Without father, without mother, without descent, having neither beginning of days, nor end of life; but made like unto the Son of God; abides a priest continually" **(Hebrews chapter 7:3) (KJV)**

(My emphasis) what kind of human being is this? No father, no mother, without descent, having no beginning of days, nor end of life...? Why is he telling us these things? Why all these explanations? What is he trying to tell us? He is trying to tell us that Melchizedek was a type of Jesus, or that Jesus is a type of Melchizedek, either way you look at it. He is telling us that Melchizedek collected tithe of all from Abraham and that we not only have another Priest who is the same as Melchizedek, but one who is greater.

He is trying to tell us that the man Abraham, who got justification by his faith towards God, gave a tithe of all to a Priest whose origin or descent we knew nothing about, he only appeared out of the blues once and never to be seen again. How much more do we who also have been justified by our faith in God through Jesus, present our tithes and offerings to the One to whom the entire Bible is written concerning? He is drawing a correlation by saying the priest that collected tithe from Abraham was the Priest of the Most High God and that his Priesthood abides forever. (He isn't a temporary Priest like that of the Levitical priests, but a Priest forever. The era of the Levitical priesthood is past because they were temporal, but the Priest of the Most High God remains forever, and because he lives forever, the order of his Priesthood still stands and will not change though that of men had to be replaced). Now I want you to imagine this: what if the name of Jesus is Melchizedek instead? Wouldn't we have concluded that, oh yes, he collected tithe from Abraham therefore we have no excuse not to give him our tithes as already been shown to us?

"Now consider how great this man was, unto whom even the patriarch Abraham gave the tenth of the spoils. And verily they that are of the sons of Levi, who receive the office of the priesthood, have a commandment to take tithes of the people according to the law, that is, of their brethren, though they come out of the loins of Abraham" **(Hebrews chapter 7:4-6) (KJV)** (My emphasis) consider how great this man was...; exactly how great was Melchizedek? Let's find out.

"The Lord has taken an oath and will not break his vow: You are a priest forever in the order of Melchizedek" **(Psalms chapter 110:4, Hebrews chapter 5:6, Hebrews chapter 5:10, Hebrews chapter 6:20, Hebrews chapter 7:17, Hebrews chapter 7:21) (NLT)**. According to the Bible, Melchizedek's greatness has no equal until the arrival of our Lord Jesus Christ. Whom when he came, the Bible had no one to compare him to but his predecessor, Melchizedek. Now here is the thing. Had Abraham being alive during the time of our Lord Jesus Christ, he would have most gladly rejoiced to repeat the same thing he did to Melchizedek and even more if need be. There would not have been any confusion or contradiction on the issue of giving tithe to Jesus the High Priest, the only One that mediates between mankind and God.

But here is the most interesting thing and implication of Abraham paying tithe to Melchizedek. He foresaw Jesus the High Priest Himself in the shadow of Melchizedek that faithful day he returned in victory over his enemies. God fast forwarded him in time to see our Lord Jesus and when he recognised him, he rejoiced and gave a tenth of all. The Bible will go on to say in the book of **John chapter 8:56:** "Your father Abraham rejoiced to see my day: and he saw it, and was glad." The day Abraham's life changed was that faithful day he encountered Melchizedek (Jesus) on his way from battle. The Lord opened his eyes to behold the grandeur of the One that is to come, the High Priest Himself, Jesus Christ the Son of God, and he reverenced and gave a tithe of all and was blessed forever.

How did I figure this? I know this because it is evident there is no other person in heaven or on earth that has that title other than Jesus as I mentioned earlier. The only person that had no beginning of days and ending of life is God himself and we know according to the Scriptures that Jesus and the Father are one. Every other being were created; including the angels and cherubim's, God created them all. They all have beginnings and God can silence them forever whenever He chooses to. There cannot, and it is practically impossible for two kings to rule and reign in the same domain. So why should there be King Melchizedek and King Jesus in the same sphere, and with the same title, King of Peace and Priest of the Most High God? That is not the case: it was Jesus who came down in the title of Melchizedek for to justify Abraham, in that he heard the same gospel we are hearing today and believed, and God credited it to him as righteousness, just as we all have been justified by the atoning blood of Jesus today.

Thus, "without all contradiction the less is blessed of the better. And here men that die receive tithes; but *there* he received them, of whom it is witnessed that he lives. And as I may so say, Levi also, who received tithes, payed tithes in Abraham. For he was yet in the loins of his father, when Melchizedek met him" (**Hebrews chapter 7:7-10**)

Here is the end of all contradictions and arguments: here men that die receive tithes, but there he receives them, of whom it is witnessed that he lives. "Of whom it is witnessed that he lives." Who on earth could the Bible be referring to? He is referring to the One of whom it is said, "The Lord has sworn and will not repent. You are a Priest forever after the order of Melchizedek." The book of Hebrews stressed that if men of the Old Testament gave tithes to the Levitical priests that were mortals, how much more, should they give to our heavenly Priest which is Jesus Christ, the one that is alive forevermore? The one who started by collecting tithe the very first time he appeared on the scene? He has not changed, though the Testament or Covenant had to.

Chapter fifteen: Offerings and free will offerings

Some say the only thing we are now required to do in terms of giving is to give a free-will offering not tithes, as New Testament believers; citing **2 Corinthians chapter 9:7** as their basis. However, a close look at this passage suggests this passage is talking about an entirely different kind offering. So let us look at this passage from the first verse.

"For as touching the ministering to the saints. It is superfluous for me to write to you" **(2 Corinthians chapter 9:1) (KJV)**. Apostle Paul was saying to the Corinthian believers there was no need for him to remind them about ministering to the saints knowing they were always more than eager and ready to give to the saints. Mark the word ministering to the saints. In this he said they should do it cheerfully and as each of them purposed in their hearts.

Now the question is, is ministering to saints all we are required to do as believers? Is that all we are required to do in terms of giving? What about ministering to the poor, the widows and widowers, strangers, orphans, the sick? Not to mention church leaders even though it is also in the category of saints. What about maintenance of the place of worship or place of gathering, where will those come from? Now let us assume all we are expected to do is for everyone to give as him or her has purposed to in their hearts, how much do you put in the offering basket when you go to church on Sunday or during midweek service? You may be putting in a lot of money into the offering basket but what about your neighbour, do you have an idea how much they put in if they did put in at all? Have we ever considered there is something called the "house of God" where God's children goes to pray and seek the face of God? **(Matthew chapter 21:13)**

Large portion of the book of Ezra was about men of the Old Testament who dedicated their time, energy and resources in rebuilding the house of God and these men where men of the not so better Testament, how much more should we of the better Testament do, in ensuring the house of our God does not lay in ruin, or worst still vanish altogether? The Church is the house of God as we understand from **1 Timothy chapter 3:15** that says, "So that if I am delayed, you will know how people must conduct themselves in the household of God. This is the church of the living God, which is the pillar and foundation of the truth" So if we claim that we are better and superior than the people of the Old Testament due to the work our Lord Jesus did, where then is the proof? Oh yes! We have got to show the proof for it. Or have we suddenly forgotten that to whom much is given, much is equally expected? **(Luke chapter 12:48)** If we truly believe that Christ has done so much for us as we claim, what is ten percent of our wage or profit, in reciprocation to such love in other to expand his kingdom and further His Gospel? I guess it is nothing in comparison.

Chapter sixteen: Three levels of tithing your pastor probably never told you about

(i) God's tithes: (Leviticus 27:30-31)

"One-tenth of the produce of the land, whether grain from the fields or fruit from the trees, belongs to the Lord and must be set apart to him as holy. If you want to buy back the Lord's tenth of the grain or fruit, you must pay its value, plus 20 percent." **(NLT)**

(ii) Tithe for oneself: (Deuteronomy chapter 14:22-26)

You must set aside a tithe of your crops-one-tenth of all the crops you harvest each year. Bring this tithe to the designated place of worship-the place the Lord your God chooses for his name to be honored-and eat it there in his presence. This applies to your tithes of grain, new wine, olive oil, and the firstborn makes of your flocks and herds. Doing this will teach you always to fear the Lord your God. Now when the Lord your God blesses you with a good harvest, the place of worship he chooses for his name to be honored might be too far for you to bring the tithe. If so, you may sell the tithe portion of your crops and herds, put the money in a pouch, and go to the

place the Lord your God has chosen.
When you arrive, you may use the money
to buy any kind of food you want-
cattle, sheep, goats, wine, or other
alcoholic drink. Then feast there in
the presence of the Lord your God and
celebrate with your household. **(NLT)**

(iii) Special dedicated welfare tithe: (Deuteronomy chapter 14:27-29)

And do not neglect the Levites in
your town, for they will receive no
allotment of land among you. At the end
of every third year, bring the entire
tithe of that year's harvest and store
it in the nearest town. Give it to the
Levites, who will receive no allotment
of land among you, as well as to the
foreigners living among you, the
orphans, and the widows in your towns,
so they can eat and be satisfied. Then
the Lord your God will bless you in all
your work. **(NLT)**

Proverbs chapter 3:9-10 "Honor the
Lord with your wealth and with the best
part of everything you produce. Then
he will fill your barns with grain, and
your vats will overflow with good
wine." **(NLT)**

Tithing is one of the ways God is
using to test our loyalty to him. The
tithe He asked us to pay does not
physically go to heaven where He uses

them to buy whatever He desires. He does not need our money in that regard. However, the tithe has some spiritual implications which are that it is connected to souls been worn to the kingdom of God and also for men to experience the touch of God upon them through the believer's generosity. How? The men and women who answered God's call on a full time assignment and has no other means of livelihood should be carted for by someone. And that someone is God through you and I, who are been fed spiritual food by them. These are the words of Apostle Paul to the Corinthians...

1 Corinthians chapter 9:4-14 "Don't we have the right to live in your homes and share your meals? Don't we have the right to bring a believing wife with us as the other apostles and the Lord's brothers do, and as Peter does? Or is it only Barnabas and I who have to work to support ourselves? What soldier has to pay his own expenses? What farmer plants a vineyard and doesn't have the right to eat some of its fruit? What shepherd cares for a flock of sheep and isn't allowed to drink some of the milk? Am I expressing merely a human opinion, or does the law say the same thing? For the Law of Moses says, you must not muzzle an ox to keep it from eating as it treads out the grain. Was God thinking only about oxen when he said this? Wasn't he actually speaking to us? Yes, it was written for us, so that the one who plows and the one who threshes the grain might both expect a share of the harvest. Since we have planted spiritual seed among you, aren't we entitled to a harvest of physical food and drink? If you support others who preach to you, shouldn't we have an even greater right to be supported? But we have never used this right. We would rather put up with anything than be an obstacle to the Good News about Christ. Don't you realize that those who work in the temple get their meals from the offerings brought to the temple? And those who serve at the altar get a share of the sacrificial offerings. In the same way, the Lord ordered that those who preach the Good News should be supported by those who benefit from it." **(NLT)**

The very last sentence he made in verse fourteen is very important and it says, "In the same way, the Lord ordered that those who preach the Good News should be supported by those who benefit from it." So you see, God already made plans for the people that preach the gospel and one of the ways He intends to carter for them is through His blessings upon our lives as Christians, not as unbelievers. And the question is, will you and I deny Him what is due Him by withholding and not giving? Please note: the above passage may not be talking about tithing per se, but one clear thing is that God has made provisions for His servants through our giving or through our monies and whether it is through tithing or through offering either way we owe it to God via paying it through the church as a proxy. Even here Apostle Paul quoted what the law says in **Deuteronomy 25:4,** reminding them that God wasn't necessarily talking about oxen only, but that He also had us in mind, we the saints of the New Covenant. In this he said those things were written for our sakes. Thereby validating all the questions that has been raised and answered in this book. Also, Apostle Paul had no right to quote a single statement from the Law of Moses, if our Lord Jesus Christ has nullified the law according to those who argue we should not pay tithes.

By God's grace since I became a Christian and understood what the Bible says about tithing I have never looked back by defaulting and God is my witness, and I have never lacked even when I had no job or means of income. God always mysteriously provided all my needs. God has really made life so easy for me by giving me the things I never thought I was able to achieve in life. However, these are not the reason I give, so I can be blessed, but I give and do those things as an act of obedience and any blessings I receive as a result of my obedience is an added bonus.

Secondly, God intends for us to enjoy life by setting aside some time and the victuals to make merry whilst we are alive. Some Christians work round the clock without resting or take care of their basic necessities; this is unacceptable to God. The Bible says that God rested on the seventh day from all His works **Genesis chapter 2:2**. This is an indication of how we too should live our lives to create time of rest from all our works. It is only when we rest that our energy and strength to continue life are renewed: but when we don't, our bodies get tired and becomes susceptible to all kinds of sicknesses and diseases. I used to be like this in the past, working round the clock without resting or buy anything descent to eat or wear until the Lord started to open my eyes to some of this truth. Today when I get my wage from my labour what I do first is to take thirty percent out and divide it into three parts. One part is for God which I pay to the church, the second part is for me to buy whatever my heart desires to buy and enjoy life whilst I live, and the third part is set aside to help people and this is where the special dedicated welfare tithe comes in play.

Thirdly, God wants us to always have something ready for the poor, the needy, the strangers, the homeless, the widows, orphans, and the sick; those disadvantaged in the society and to always ensure there is enough provision in His house ready for anyone who might need them. You see, in the past I found it hard to give to the poor person on the street when they ask for money. The reasons for that was because I used to think if I should give them money they would spend it on buying drugs and my money would be a source of harm instead blessing to them. More so, should they be legitimate beggars the truth was that I never made any provisions to that effect. But today, as soon as I see a beggar or a homeless person, I never waited for them to ask me for money before giving them, and that is because I had initially made provisions for them by setting aside a percentage of my wage in advance. (How do I do it? I change notes into lots of coins in advance) This was thanks to the day I heard our pastor encouraging us to not relent in giving to the poor due to what we think they would do with the money. But instead we should give in response to obedience to the word of God. Once we have given, heaven will record that we have done our part and whatever they decides to do with the money is left between them and God.

Chapter seventeen: Tithe, part of God's master design

"Think again, you fools! When will you finally catch on? Is he deaf-the one who made your ears? Is he blind-the one who formed your eyes? He punishes the nations-won't he also punish you? He knows everything-doesn't he also know what you are doing? The Lord knows people's thoughts; he knows they are worthless!" **(Psalms chapter 94:8-11). (NLT)**

The God we are dealing with is a Master architect and builder. The implication of this statement is that God is Omniscient. He knows all things that can be perceived; and everything beyond the scope of our limited minds and imaginations. There is no thought of man that can go without the knowledge of this Great God. The reason is that He is the Master of every design both Arts, Science, Technology, Math, Geography, Chemistry, Engineering and any other discipline you can think of.

I would like you to take a moment to ruminate over the great work of God from creation. The Bible says that God spoke the world into existence by simply saying "Let there be...," and instantly, whatever He called appeared. Think about the man He created, the entire different compositions and anatomy of the human body which overall formed a living being: which includes all animals, fishes and the birds. Ever wondered how the human brain functions? What about the heart that pumps and circulates blood within the body? What about the kidney that filters the blood and removes toxic substances out of the body? What about the gut that hosts billions of bacteria? The small and large intestine, the veins and arteries in the body? What about the reflexes? Stimulus, senses, the human mind and all the various organs in the body? Have you ever sat down to ask how all of these synchronise together to make a human being become a living soul? Everything works in perfect harmony as they were ordained by God.

David said, "O Lord, you have examined my heart and know everything about me. You know when I sit down or stand up. You know my thoughts even when I'm far away. You see me when I travel and when I rest at home. You know everything I do. You know what I am going to say even before I say it, Lord. You go before me and follow me. You place your hand of blessing on my head. Such knowledge is too wonderful for me, too great for me to understand." **(Psalms chapter 139:1-6) (NLT)**

God is awesome. He is the one that made it all. Is it possible, without any part of the human body, man would be any different? Why did He gave us two legs, two hands, two ears, two eyes and almost everything in pair? Why? What would happen if we only have one leg, a hand, an ear or a single eye? I am sure you know what the answer is. We will not be perfect. But with everything the way we are, He looked at His creation and said "They are good." Everything has a purpose. The same goes to the doctrines of God including tithes and offerings.

Tithe and offering were not ordained by accident, just as none of the human body was mistakenly added. Tithe was not ordained by accident in the Old Testament only to be discovered it is imperfect and needed making redundant in the New Testament, just as none of God's master piece designs is imperfect and needs removing at any time. Neither ordained He them by mistake, or as a way of wishful thinking. Tithing is part of God's design, God who is the master architect and builder of all things. He built them all for an enduring reason and purpose. The entire Bible, every story, history, doctrine, law, prophecy, obedience, disobedience, faith, weakness and strength were all cleverly knitted together piece by piece, by the Everlasting Father to give glory to Him, and to Him alone.

Chapter eighteen: Jesus did not abolish the law, he fulfilled it instead

"Think not that I am come to destroy the law, or the prophets: I am not come to destroy, but to fulfill. For verily I say unto you. Till heaven and earth pass, one jot or one title shall in no wise pass from the law, till all be fulfilled. Whosoever therefore shall break one of these least commandments and shall teach men so, he shall be called the least in the kingdom of heaven: but whosoever shall do and teach them, the same shall be called great in the kingdom of heaven. For I say unto you, that except your righteousness shall exceed the righteousness of the Scribes and Pharisees, ye shall in no case enter into the kingdom of heaven." **(Matthew chapter 5:17-20) KJV)**

People's arguments as to why we are no longer required to pay tithes is the fact they assume we no longer have anything to do with the law. That as far as Christianity is concerned, Christ has delivered us from the law. But are they right or wrong? I personally believe we are still yoked with the law indirectly whether we like it, know it, or not. We cannot escape the law.

Think not that I am come to destroy the law, or the prophets: I am not come to destroy, but to fulfill **(Matthew chapter 5:17)**. These are the words of Jesus, our Captain, our Lord and Master. The one whose voice we listen to and follow whatever he says. He said he did not come to abolish the law or the prophets. What does it mean to abolish something? To abolish means to bring to an end or to destroy an existing agreement. No, he said no that is not what he came to do neither did he came to destroy all the beautiful works the prophets had done in the past. No, instead they are all fulfilled in him. Not that they all stopped in him. To demonstrate this, he asked the leper whom he had healed to go and show himself to the priest and offer the gifts commanded by Moses. **Matthew chapter 8:4** (My emphasis) if he had come to put an end to the law and stop us from doing anything the law requires us to do, why then would he ask the leper to go show himself to the priest and offer whatever sacrifices Moses commanded?

So if our assumption was that the ordinance of tithe is part of the law, now we can clearly see that Jesus did not destroy the law and in-fact he endorses it. Else he would not have asked the leper to go show himself to the priests. Brethren Jesus did not destroy the Law as there were no need for him to do so, and come to think of

112

it, the laws were his own words that will 'not pass away.'

For verily I say unto you. Till heaven and earth pass, one jot or one title shall in no wise pass from the law, till all be fulfilled. **(Matthew chapter 5:18).** (My emphasis) the word "Till heaven and earth pass away," is a strong statement. It was Jesus's way of saying the law will not pass away, and that we are all still yoked with the law until the day he presents the Church which is his Bride to the Father without spot or wrinkle. Just in case you missed what he said, read again; "one jot or one title shall in no wise pass from the law, till all be fulfilled." Those arguing we are not to pay tithe because it is an Old Testament Law, what does this verse say to you? Do these words of Jesus by anyway suggest it has ended or no longer relevant? I pray that God himself will grant you more understanding in Jesus name!

"Whosoever therefore shall break one of these least commandments and shall teach men so, he shall be called the least in the kingdom of heaven: but whosoever shall do and teach them, the same shall be called great in the kingdom of heaven." **(Matthew chapter 5:19)** (My emphasis) this is a warning to all those that are arguing and teaching others not to pay tithe that they are doing themselves a huge

113

disfavour. And unless they repent, they will stand before God at the last day and give account of their deeds.

We cannot fault God's laws no matter how imperfect they may appear before God. We are not Gods, we are His subjects that do his bidding. **Psalms chapter 19:7** says that the law of the Lord is perfect. So I want to ask you that is reading this book, do you pay your tithes? Have you stopped paying because people on the internet are saying we should not pay tithe? Or are you one of those that are kicking against the paying of tithe? I want you to repent today before it is too late. You cannot fight against God nobody can. The Bible says in the book of **Matthew chapter 21:44** "And whosoever shall fall on this stone shall be broken: but on whomsoever it shall fall, it will grind to powder." Do not let the wrath of the Almighty God fall on you. Repent and mend your ways before it is too late. Our Lord Jesus said 'anybody that shall break the smallest of the commandments of the Law and teach men to do so shall be least in the Kingdom of God. I pray you will not be counted as least on the day you face your maker in Jesus name.

"For I say unto you. That except your righteousness shall exceed the righteousness of the Scribes and Pharisees, ye shall in no case enter into the kingdom of heaven." **(Matthew chapter 5:20). (KJV)**

Except our righteousness exceeds that of the Scribes and Pharisees? Who are these people, the Scribes and the Pharisees? Here is a glimpse of who they are.

"The Pharisee stood and prayed thus with himself. God, I thank thee, that I am not as other men are, extortioners, unjust, adulterers, or even as this publican. I fast twice in the week, I give tithes of all that I possess." **(Luke chapter 18:11-12). (KJV)**

The Scribes and Pharisees were those that understood the law even though they did not follow everything it said, which was why Jesus was always at a loggerhead with them. They were the custodians of the law, for they knew it inside out. Not only that, they never defaulted in their tithes as indicated in the above passage. But yet, Jesus told them, "Woe unto you, Scribes and Pharisees, hypocrites! For ye pay tithe of mint and anise and cumin, and have omitted the weightier matters of the law, judgment, mercy, and faith: these ought ye to have done, and not to leave the other undone." **(Matthew chapter 23:23)** (My emphasis) Jesus wants us to do more in terms of good works. He wants our deeds to surpass and to go beyond that of those who claim to know the law and yet do not follow the law.

He wants us to go the extra miles in bearing fruits, conducts and relationship with God and with man. The Scribes and Pharisees where good at paying some tithes, but defaulted in terms of judgment and showing mercy to others and Jesus rebuked them that they should not only just pay tithes, but should also continue in doing judgment, showing mercy and having more faith in God. So if somebody is preaching you should not pay tithes they are preaching it so you can follow them in disobeying God's command, not necessarily because they love you, but on the contrary, they hate you and want you to be as disobedient as they are.

If our Lord Jesus said except our righteousness surpasses the ones of the Scribes and the Pharisees, we have no chance of seeing the kingdom of God. Won't it be a good idea for us to study and understand who these groups of people are? By the way, was our Lord Jesus confused when he made those comments? Or did he just say those words because he likes to talk and condemn people? Did he say those words not having us, today's Christians in mind? The Pharisee prayed and said, 'oh Father, I thank you that I do not commit adultery, I'm not unjust and I'm not an extortioner. I pray and fast twice a week and I pay all my tithes.'

Amongst the list of things this Pharisee mentioned, which one of them are we not required to do as believers in Christ? Why are we expected to do everything, but tithe? What is it with tithe that made us hate it so much? I know the answer to that: it is because there is money involved, and we do not like parting with our hard-earned monies, myself included. A Christian will do all he can not to extort another person. He will flee faster than Joseph not to commit adultery, and he will do forty days dry fasting with intense prayers to defeat the forces of darkness, but when it comes to money, it becomes a different ball game. We look for scriptures that justifies every other doctrine, but condemns only tithe. This should not be so. We should learn to reverence every bit of God's word and as we do so, He will see our desires to be obedient and aid us when we miss any, instead of arguing and twisting His word.

"Blessed is the man who walks not in the counsel of the ungodly, nor stands in the path of sinners, nor sits in the seat of the scornful; But his delight is in the law of the Lord; and in his law he meditates day and night. He shall be like a tree planted by the rivers of water, that brings forth its fruit in his season, whose leaf also shall not wither; and whatever he does shall prosper." **(Psalms chapter 1:1-3). (NKJV)**

"My son, if sinners entice you, do not consent." **(Proverbs chapter 1:10). (NKJV).** The Bible is admonishing us to be wise, not to be so foolish as to allow anybody to deceive us with their own invented doctrines. And the question is, will you allow yourself to be deceived and become a victim? A word is enough for the wise. The Bible says "him that has an ear let him hear what the Spirit is saying unto the churches" **(Revelation chapter 2:29)** and the word of God is that Spirit according to **John chapter 6:63** "It is the Spirit who gives life; the flesh profits nothing. The words that I speak to you are spirit, and they are life" **(NKJV)**

The only time Jesus mentioned tithe was when he rebuked the Scribes and Pharisees that they should not have done the one and leave the other undone. But one thing was clear; he said "I have yet many things to say unto you but you cannot bear them now. However, when He, the Spirit of truth has come, He will guide you into all truth: for He shall not speak of Himself; but whatsoever He shall hear, that shall He speak: and He will show you things to come." **(John chapter 16:12-13)** (My emphasis) Jesus told his disciples to anticipate the coming of the Holy Spirit who will guide and teach them all things. Today we have the Holy Spirit and what is the Spirit saying to the Church?

Now the Spirit speaketh expressly, "That in the latter times some shall depart from the faith, giving heed to seducing spirits, and doctrines of devils; speaking lies in hypocrisy; having their conscience seared with hot iron; forbidding to marry and commanding to abstain from meats, which God hath created to be received with thanksgiving of them which believe and know the truth. **("1 Timothy chapter 4:1-3) (KJV)**. (My emphasis). The Spirit cannot be wrong it is not possible. The God that knows the end from the beginning already fore-knew the times we are in, in this generation; and He has forewarned us that some will depart from the faith through paying attention to the doctrines of seducing spirits. These doctrines are lies from the pits of hell, cleverly coated to entice and suit the ears of the hearers, with the aim of deceiving and gaining more followers to themselves. Brethren we are at the latter times and the days are full of evil. All kinds of demons and evil seducing spirits have been unleashed to deceive even the very elect and our only saving grace is to hold tight to the doctrines of our profession.

Chapter nineteen: What happens when God's children refuse to pay their tithe?

"I will build my church, and the gates of hell shall not prevail against it." (Matthew chapter 16:18) (KJV)

One certain thing about the Church of God is this; the gates of hell has been on a constant battle right from the onset till now, and will continue till the Church is raptured, to prevail or overcome it. The reason for this, is that the Church is the only element posing a threat to the kingdom of darkness. In the book of **Mark gospel chapter 3:27** the Bible says, "No man can enter into a strong man's house and spoil his goods, except he will first bind the strong man: and then he'll spoil his house".

This passage shows us that the kingdom of God only came to liberate men and women who were held bound in darkness by the devil in this world. However, the strong man which is the devil is not folding his hands and watch his kingdom be defeated without putting up a fight. A battle line was drawn after Jesus defeated the kingdom of darkness and handed the victory to his Church to continue. Since then, all the devil is interested in doing is to stop the Church from progressing; from advancing, from preaching the good news to those in captivity and delivering those under the bondage of sin.

Luke chapter 4:18 "The Spirit of the Lord is upon me, because he hath anointed me to preach the gospel to the poor; he hath sent me to heal the broken hearted, to preach deliverance to the captives, and recovering of sight to the blind, to set at liberty them that are bruised. To preach the acceptable year of the lord"

The assignment Jesus came to do over two thousand years ago is the same mandate handed over to the Church. Now here is an interesting thing to note. Because of this mandate was Jesus silenced, crucified, killed and buried, so he would not preach the acceptable year of the Lord. Because of this mandate were the Apostles persecuted, imprisoned, forbidden and martyred, so they do not succeed in preaching the acceptable year of the Lord. All these were done by the devil through human mediums. It did not end there with the Apostles, it is the same reason he has been sabotaging the church via every means possible today. And all the voices raging via different platforms, disputing, and kicking against tithing, which is the only means of the Church Jesus died for, to be sustained and maintained whilst carrying on, on that mandate, are the same voices that cried, "Crucify him, Crucify him" (**Luke chapter 23:21**)

Christ is building his church here on earth not in heaven. In heaven when the church would have been raptured: what Christ would do will be to present her as a bride to the Father; but for now here on earth what he is doing is building. Thus, if Christ is building his church, and we his Bride refuse to pay tithe with which Church buildings are sustained and maintained and churches are shut down, how is it that we are building with him? The Bible says "he that does not gather with me scatters..." (**Matthew chapter 12:30**)

The first thing that will happen should God's children desist from paying their tithes is that churches will close down one after the other. Secondly, sinners will not be saved because labourers will diminish and there will not be anybody to preach to them.

"How then shall they call on him in whom they have not believed? And how shall they believe in him of whom they have not heard? And how shall they hear without a preacher? And how shall they preach, except they be sent? As it is written, how beautiful are the feet of them that preach the gospel of peace, and bring glad tidings of good things." (**Romans chapter 10:14-15**)

The third thing that will happen is that the fate of the world Jesus died for will be worse than it is now, as darkness will envelop it. What would be left would be for the speedy return of the Lord, who will not bear to see the world in such a state. Now should all that were mentioned above take place, who do we honestly think will be held accountable? You guessed right if you said that wicked servant who refused to use the talent of money given to him to yield increase that would benefit his master according to **Matthew chapter 25:14-30.** The soul of one sinner is far greater than all the money in this world put together. Hence, our Lord Jesus Christ stopped at nothing, including dying on the cross for them (us). How can we that call Jesus our Lord and Master, refuse to give a fraction from all he has given us in other to support his assignment of soul winning, be able to lay claim of anything in his kingdom?

Chapter twenty: What should the church do with the tithe?

Since we have established the fact that tithing is God's command and an obligation for every true Christian, I guess the biggest legitimate question we should be asking is, what does God expect the church to use it for? I am using the word 'Church' here instead of 'Pastor' for a reason. The Church is bigger than any one single individual regardless of their title or position. The Church is the collection of the gathered believers; and the Head of the Church is Christ, not the Pope, G.O, Pastor, Evangelist, Prophet or Apostle.

The reason there's tithe mismanagement or financial misappropriation by leaders is because some think they are the head of the Church of Christ. They think they are the ones that should and must have the last say on issues and matters in the Church. They think every money which comes in is for them and their family since they are the Church leaders: but they are very wrong. Ever wondered why it is only the leader of the Church or Ministry that are always the ones who enjoy most of the luxuries? All the cars, private jets, houses, large bank accounts and huge salaries? This is due to the mind set of some church leaders and their congregation. If that is not

the case there would have been
instances of where the assistant
Pastors and others within the
leadership hierarchy also possess
private jets and all the other luxuries
mentioned above, but no. This is the
reason so much is lavished on a single
person and at the end eyebrows are
raised and people starts to question
and query why a single so-called
servant of God should amass so much
wealth to him or herself? Therefore,
everybody wants to be a big Church
leader and at the end even those not
called, and the devils agents got
muddled up together and it becomes hard
to distinguish those that are real and
those that are not. Let us consider
Acts chapter 2:44-47

"And all that believed were
together and had all things common; and
sold their possessions and goods, and
parted them to all men, as every man
had need. And they continued daily with
one accord in the temple, and breaking
bread from house to house, did eat
their meat with gladness and
singleness of heart, praising God, and
having favour with all the people. And
the Lord added to the church daily such
as should be saved." (My emphasis)

This passage alone speaks volume on
how funds that come into the church
whether through tithe, freewill
offering, seed or any other means
should be viewed and distributed. It

is important first and foremost to note that money *must* come into the church one way or the other as the Lord moves the hearts and minds of people to give in response to the blessings and love of God. For the kingdom of God to reach the ends of the world, both money and human resources are an indispensable means and tools for it to be done successfully.

Therefore, going back to the Old Testament, God had to introduce the various means via which this can be achieved, and part of that was through tithes and freewill offerings. Now, the primary reason tithe was linked or associated with the law though it is not part of the law as it predates it, was to sustain the Levites whom God assigned to be in charge of the services and duties of the tabernacle. Reason been they were not to have other sources of livelihood. But that was in the Old Testament. The Testament we understood was faulted by God in **Acts chapter 8:8**. So again, we see that if provisions was made for an imperfect Testament, so to say; to support those that ministered in it, how much more provisions then, should be allocated towards the New and better Testament?

Again, what should the church do with the tithe and offerings that come in? Well, since no specific direct directions and instructions are made by our Lord Jesus about this, what do we do? But, Oh! I remember that though our Lord Jesus did not elaborate on tithing, what about the One he said he was going to send that will teach us all things? Is the Holy Spirit yet to mention anything concerning how to use the money that comes into the house of God?

"But the comforter, which is the Holy Ghost, whom the Father will send in my name, he shall teach you all things, and bring all things to your remembrance, whatsoever I have said unto you" **(John chapter 14:26)**.

One important question we must ask ourselves that will help unlock this answer is this, is it possible that the all-knowing God, the One we're to safely assume foreknew all the arguments and debates the church is facing now concerning this issue hasn't said anything whatsoever regarding the issue of tithe and what it should be used for in our dispensation? I do not think so. One thing we can understand about God the Father, God the Son and God the Holy Spirit is that their mode of communication and dealings with us are different, just as the three different eras the world has witnessed about the Almighty Father differs from each other. But though their modes of communications differ, yet they are in total harmony with each other instead of contradicting each other. The Son did not contradict anything the Father previously say, neither did the Holy Spirit contradict anything spoken by the Father or the Son. They all both agree with each other. "For there are three that bear record in heaven, the Father, the Word, and the Holy Ghost: and these three are one" **(1 John chapter 5:7)**.

"God, who at sundry times and in divers manners spake in time past unto the fathers by the prophets, hath in these last days spoken unto us by his Son, whom he hath appointed heir of all things, by whom also he made the worlds;" **(Hebrews chapter 1:1-2)**

It is not the aim of this book to point out all the different times and ways the entirety of the Godhead has and is still manifesting Himself to His children, but one thing that is certain is that God spoke to the fathers in the Old Testament invisibly, through audible voices, through angelic visitations, and through dreams and visions. When Jesus came to the scene he spoke to the people visibly and rebuked his hearers for the hardness of their hearts. Today, the Holy Spirit is speaking to us in divers forms such as through visitations, dreams, visions, revelations, inner witness, and remembrance of what has been said in the past, to explain it in a way we can understand them.

"Then he said unto them, O fools, and slow of heart to believe all that the prophets have spoken: Ought not Christ to have suffered these things, and to enter into his glory? And beginning at Moses and all the prophets, he expounded unto them in all the scriptures the things concerning himself... And their eyes were opened, and they knew him: and he vanished out of their sight. And they said one to another, did not our heart burn within us, while he talked with us by the way, and while he opened to us the scriptures? **(Luke chapter 24:25-27; verse 30-31)**

The Holy Spirit has already shown us what to do with every resource that comes into the house of God, the Church; and if we truly have Him inside of us, there'd be a strong witness and convictions concerning not just what to do with the tithe, but also the validity of paying it in the first place.

Thus, the Lord desires us to have all things in common in regard to the income that comes into His house to the point of parting it with those that have needs. Not hoarding it to lavish on a single individual called the pastor, or to build a mega structure called mega church. I think that is a waste of God's resources as many are going hungry whilst sitting in the midst of such great wealth.

I understand that church business is a big business, but a big kingdom business. In this business a lot of money will come in every now and again which the Lord expects the servants He has placed in charge to diligently distribute for the advancement of His kingdom. And I know most churches are doing a lot of charity works across the globe some of which are unheard-of, and which they cannot go and start broadcasting for people to know about. However, I am convinced, a lot more still needs to be done. Things like building free schools for the less privileged to attend without paying a cent. Free medical facilities where the poor can gain access to free medical treatments. Things like partnering with other churches who are unable to afford paying the rent of their church facility let alone paying salaries to their full-time pastors and many more. I think these would be a very good way to appropriate God's resources and if they are done, even those that are paying the tithes will know and also see that their tithes are being used for a good cause. But it is only when they are been used inappropriately that people starts to raise eyebrows and the devil steps in to expose them thereby bringing reproach to the kingdom of God.

Chapter twenty one: Our errors in response to the errors of others

One of the key reason many people conclude not to pay their tithes is this; they say things like, "These Pastors are greedy and selfish. They live extravagantly while their congregations live from hand-to-mouth...," and many other reasons which they think are legitimate enough to stop them from being obedient to faithfully pay their tithes to God.

Firstly, may I use this opportunity to congratulate all genuine Pastors and servants of God out there; who labour day and night, both in good and bad times to ensure the kingdom of God is marching forward, despite everything the enemy is throwing at the Church. Please be encouraged, your reward awaits you for certain, and nothing can take it away from you. Because faithful is he who made the promise, who also will do it in Jesus name. My prayer is for the Lord to keep you going as He has always done until we see Him face to face.

Secondly, it is important for other Pastors who themselves are guilty one way or the other of misappropriating Gods money: to carefully take some moment to reflect on these reasons many are saying is why they will not pay tithes as a result of their conduct, to desist from their ways and repent for the Lord to forgive them before it becomes too late. Here is what our Lord Jesus said concerning that man or woman that will cause any of his children to be offended:

"But whoso shall offend one of these little ones which believe in me, it were better for him that a millstone were hanged about his neck, and that he were drowned in the depth of the sea. Woe unto the world because of offences! For it must needs be that offences come: but woe to that man by whom the offence cometh!" **(Matthew chapter 18:6-7)**

So Pastor, or whatever title you may have been given: let this warning be a wakeup call to you. The Lord is taking note of your actions and attitudes towards what belongs to Him, and He will not hold you guiltless if you continue to cause many to stumble. Therefore, repent before it is too late and God will always forgive and restore you back to Himself if you do so.

To you who is offended as a result of what you see these Pastors do, let these passages console you that the Lord knows all these things must come to pass and has also forewarned you well ahead of time, of days like these and it is up to you to either continue holding unto the Lord, or let go of that which you had once believed was right. This is what the Lord is saying to you.

"Unto the angel of the church of Ephesus write: these things saith he that holdeth the seven stars in his right hand, who walketh in the midst of the seven golden candlesticks: I know thy works, and thy labour, and thy patience, and how thou canst not bear them which are evil: and thou hast tried them which say they are apostles, and are not, and hast found them liars: and hast borne, and hast patience, and for my name's sake hast laboured, and hast not fainted. Nevertheless, I have somewhat against thee, because thou hast left thy first love. Remember therefore from whence thou art fallen, and repent, and do the first works: or else I will come unto thee quickly, and will remove thy candlestick out of his place, except thou repent" **(Revelation chapter 2:1-5) (KJV)**.

So, to you who is offended, I get it. There are certain human behaviours that are un-biblical such as for a man of God to have two private jets or more to himself: fleet of cars in his garage, mansions, amongst many other assets to himself alone. This leaves one to wonder, what happens to moderation?

Having said that, one of the biggest mistakes we make as believers is to make ourselves judges and juries. We become the ones that pass judgments on the things that happen in the kingdom where we are only but servants in, depriving the King Himself the honour and glory that belong to Him, who is the best Judge and Rewarder in everything that takes place under the sun. And He warns us not to condemn lest we are also condemned. There is only one Judge and His name is Jehovah, not us. As long as the Lord lives no man can escape His judgment at the end. We will all give account of our deeds on earth both the Pastors, the G.O's, the Prophets and whatever title we give ourselves. Because God is a God of justice and accountability. And He has a book wherein every deed, action and conduct are recorded and weighed. There is nothing wrong in standing to oppose evil, but once we have done so, let us move on with our own lives instead of dwelling on it and even going as far as refusing to do what we know and believe ourselves to be right in the first place.

The greatest error and harm a Christian can do to themselves, is to allow other people's rebelliousness towards God cause them to also rebel against God their maker. And I believe that is the greatest deception against a believer who ought to know better. The Bible says we should be wise as serpents and as gentle as doves. If the reason we refuse to pay our tithes is due to what we see the Pastors do with them, it is like saying I will also become a thief because the Pastor is a thief. Or I will also commit adultery or fornication because the Pastor is committing them themselves.

Today one of the ways the devil is using to unleash war against the Church is through the internet, as good as that platform is. And what he does is to position greedy men as Pastors. Men who knew nothing about the God they claim to represent and then goes on to expose their evil deeds for the world to witness and blaspheme the name of the Lord. I love the internet because all sorts of evil have been exposed through it. We have seen all kinds of deceptions, witchcraft, sorcery, bewitchment, arrogance and blasphemy against the God of heaven and all in His name by some regarded as God's servants. And one cannot really blame those people who are really standing to address and oppose these evil men and women. One thing I am against is twisting the word of God and preaching what it does not say to others just to support our arguments. That on itself is evil, and we are equally as guilty as those we are opposing. So, the Lord is asking you to remember your first love and where you have falling from. In this kingdom, there is only forward marching and not backwards marching. Because whoever puts his or her hands to the plough and looks back, the Bible says such person is not fit for the kingdom of God. So be warned. The Scripture says, "Remember where you have fallen from and do the first works"

Conclusion

"Wherefore, my beloved, as ye have always obeyed, not as in my presence only, but now much more in my absence, work out your own salvation with fear and trembling. Do all things without murmurings and disputings: that ye may be blameless and harmless, the sons of God, without rebuke, in the midst of a crooked and perverse nation, among whom ye shine as lights in the world" **(Philippians 2:12-15) (KJV)**

In **Malachi chapter 3:9** the Lord says, 'You are cursed with a curse because you have robbed me.' The Father Himself said these words not a pastor or a general overseer of one Ministry somewhere. We cannot, in this side of eternity fully understand what it means to be cursed with a curse? And I think it is a statement that is worthy to be reflected upon, especially by those who argue we should not pay our tithes. It baffles me sometimes, knowing that some Christians joke with their eternal destiny. By this I mean the chances people take knowing fully well what the word of God says, and yet disregards and teaches others to do so as well. But I thank God, it is not every Christian that is disobedient to the call to tithe but a small minority.

137

Do you know this is the only passage in the entire Bible where such statement is made? No other place in the Bible you will find such statement that somebody is cursed with a curse for not complying with God's demand.

I don't know, neither does anyone totally understands the true meaning of been cursed with a curse by God. But whatever the meaning, one thing is certain, it is not a pleasant thing. I am a human being, and one not considered intelligent by human standard, let alone to the standards of God. As a result, I cannot afford to play a game of chances with God's spoken words if I have the choice and power of will, on any giving situation. I would rather do everything I can to be on the safest side possible. If at the end of the day it meant that I went the extra miles to do what wasn't absolutely necessary for me to do in other to please God, thank God for that. It is a billion times better than coming short to be on the wrong side of judgement. As long as God gives me life and the strength to work and make ends meet, I will always honour God with my tithe. Because, come to think of it, what do I have to lose if I can afford to pay my tithe and end up paying it? There are millions of people in this world who would give everything to be in my shoes but cannot, due to poor health or as a result of lack of other privileges. May I remind you once again that God is not, and can never be mocked by anyone.

The bible says in the book of **Ecclesiastes chapter 3:14-15,** "I know that, whatsoever God does, it shall be forever: nothing can be put to it, nor anything taken from it: and God does it, that men should fear before him. That which has been is now; and that which is to be has already been; and God requires that which is past."

When I read passages in the Bible, I don't just read for reading sake; instead I try as much as I can to figure out what message is been passed, by comparing the text with other scriptures and allowing the Holy Spirit to minister to me; and then try as much as I can to put what I read into practice: which is literally doing what I read. And the word of God is so simple to understand. Only when our aims and efforts is, so we can get an extra rhema or when we try to rationalise what we have read with our human minds and senses that we miss the point. The word of God is clear and simple; and most people will agree: if you read a passage which say's thou shall not steal. There is no other revelation God will give you, or anyone else that will change the meaning. He said thou shall not steal, thus, stop stealing. 'You shall not commit adultery' meaning stop sleeping around with women, worst of all with married men or women. It is when I start to ask questions such as, does He really mean this or that? When did He say this, at what time, New or Old Testament? Just like the devil deceived Eve by asking "Did God really say, you must not eat from any tree in the garden?" (**Genesis chapter 3:1**), that is the time we miss the will of God.

When the Lord ask the people to circumcise, He meant physical circumcision and the people went ahead and circumcised themselves; because it was what was required of them. In the New dispensation, we are now told circumcision is no longer physical but spiritual. We understand that we should always try to mortify the deeds of the flesh in other to achieve spiritual circumcision. So you will agree, the word of God is simple and easy to understand. Only because men finds it hard to do the basics; that is why they ask questions and look for scriptures they think will exempt them from doing what is required.

Now, what does the word of God say in **Ecclesiastes chapter 3:14-15?** It says that everything that is happening now in our time, had happened before in the past and whatever had happened in the past will still happen again, and God requires that which is past. What is the wisdom here? The wisdom is that no amount of disobedience and apostasy to God, occurring today that is new. They have previously happened in the past, and so, nothing is new under the sun. The same way people are arguing that tithing is no longer relevant to us today is the same way the men of the Old Testament also devised a way to argue themselves out from paying; which was why God had to call them to account in Malachi chapter three. Nothing is new under the sun. Now for those who are preaching against tithing; here is what the word of God says in **Revelation chapter 22:18** "For I testify unto every man that heareth the words of the prophecy of this book, if any man shall add unto these things, God shall add unto him the plagues that are written in this book: and if any man shall take away from the words of the book of this prophecy, God shall take away his part out of the book of life, and out of the holy city, and from the things which are written in this book"

I did not say those words, they were God's words. Somebody may laugh after reading this statement that whoever wrote this book is ignorant; that the Bible was only talking about the book of Revelation and not the entire Bible. Accepted; However, the Bible also says that the testimony of Jesus is the Spirit of prophecy **(Revelation chapter 19:10)**

And so, I have come to this conclusion: the word of God is bigger than anybody to entirely understand. Both the Old and New Testament are interwoven together that it is difficult to thoroughly comprehend the dividing line. The law of God is big and beyond the comprehension of the wisest scholar. Like I said before, we cannot, and will never perfectly understand God in this side of life. Therefore, wisdom demands we play safe our arguments with fear and trembling in the assembly of believers, when giving interpretation to the things of God. Wisdom demands we seek the wisdom of the Holy Spirit before inferring, asserting or affirming what is been said in the past. Wisdom demands we argue and debate less with the thing as mysterious and majestic as the word of God. Wisdom demands we do not castigate and bring down those we think are less informed than we are. For no man is perfect, and whilst we point a finger at others, four other fingers points back at us, making us four times guiltier than the person we are pointing at. God bless you.

"Remove not the ancient landmark, which thy fathers have set." **(Proverbs 22:28) (KJV)**

About the author

An Evangelist by calling, Pastor John Okeke is a resident pastor of Christ The Vine International Pentecostal Church in Bolton, Greater Manchester UK. Obtained his Bachelor's degree in Computer Networks and Security from the University of Bolton UK; Diploma in Christian Ministry from Christ the Redeemer Bible College London. Holds a School of Disciples Certificate from Christ The Redeemer's Ministries through the RCCG and a Leadership Induction Course Certificate from the Word of Faith Bible Institute (WOFBI). Married to a Polish woman, Pastor John is a husband and a father of a pretty ten year old girl. He enjoys family and personal Bible study moments. Pastor John's vision is to empower believers with the knowledge of the power that is found in the Word of God.

Printed in Great Britain
by Amazon